DAVID WILLIAMSON was born in Me[...] brought up in Bairnsdale, north-eastern Victo[...] Mechanical Engineering from Monash Univer[...] _.. .. ..rer in thermo-dynamics and social psychology at Swinburn Institute of Technology until 1973. His first full-length play, *The Coming of Stork*, had its premiere at the La Mama Theatre, Carlton in 1970 and later became the film *Stork*, directed by Tim Burstall.

The Removalists and *Don's Party*, both written in 1971, were quickly taken up and performed around Australia, then in London and later made into films with screenplays by the author. In 1972 *The Removalists* won the Australian Writers' Guild Awgie Award for the best stage play and the best script in any medium. In 1973 David Williamson was nominated the most promising playwright by the London *Evening Standard* following the British production of *The Removalists*.

The next play was *Jugglers Three* (1972) commissioned by the Melbourne Theatre Company; followed by *What If You Died Tomorrow* (1973) for the Old Tote Theatre Company; *The Department* (1975) and *A Handful of Friends* (1976) for the South Australian Theatre Company. *The Club* (1977) broke all previous box office records and in 1978 had seasons at the Kennedy Centre, Washington, on Broadway and in Berlin. In 1980 the Nimrod Theatre production went to London. The film, directed by Bruce Beresford, was released in 1980. *Travelling North* was performed around Australia in 1979 and in London in 1980. The film version was released in 1987. It was followed by *Celluloid Heroes* (1980), *The Perfectionist* (1982), *Sons of Cain* (1985) and *Emerald City* (1987) which played in London and New York in 1988. The film version of *Emerald City* was released in 1989. *Top Silk* was first produced in Sydney and Melbourne in the same year, followed by *Siren* in 1990. *Money and Friends* was performed around Australia in 1991, in Los Angeles in 1992 and in London in 1993. *Brilliant Lies* was first produced in Brisbane in 1993 and then toured Australia. *Sanctuary* was first produced in Melbourne in 1994 and has been made into a film. *Dead White Males* was first produced in Sydney in 1995.

David Williamson has won the Australian Film Institute film script award for *Petersen* (1974), *Don's Party* (1976), *Gallipoli* (1981) and *Travelling North* (1987) and has won eleven Australian Writers' Guild Awgie Awards. He lives in Sydney with his novelist wife Kristin Williamson.

david williamson

dead white males

CURRENCY PRESS • SYDNEY

CURRENCY PLAYS
General Editor: Katharine Brisbane

First published in 1995 by
Currency Press Ltd,
PO Box 452, Paddington,
NSW, 2021, Australia

National Library of Australia Cataloguing-in-Publication data:

Williamson, David, 1942-.
 Dead white males.

ISBN 0 86819 433 3.

I. Title.

A822.3

Set by Currency, Paddington.
Printed by Southwood Press, Marrickville, NSW
Cover design by Susan Mikulic

Contents

Photographs

(p.ii) Patrick Dickson as William Shakespeare. (p.9) Above: Maggie Blinco as Grace Judd, Simon Chilvers as Col Judd, Henri Szeps as Martin Judd and Anna Volska as Sarah Judd. Below: Maggie Blinco, Michelle Doake as Angela Judd, and Babs McMillan as Monica Judd. (p.14) Henri Szeps (p.16) Above: Barbara Stephens as Jessica Squires and Michelle Doake. Below: John Howard as Grant Swain and Michelle Doake. (p.20) Patrick Dickson and Michelle Doake. (p.50) Michelle Doake and Simon Chilvers. (p.52) Glenn Hazeldine as Steve and Kelly Butler as Melissa. (p.74) Above: Kelly Butler and Simon Chilvers. Below: The cast.

Production photographs by Tracey Schramm.

Deconstructing human nature ...

David Williamson

The genesis of *Dead White Males* occurred at a literary conference some years ago when a young male academic gave a paper on deconstruction and post structuralism to a roomful of writers. No one in the room understood a word he said. When one writer rose at the end and asked for a plain English translation, we were told that it was a very difficult theory and that we shouldn't bother ourselves with it. 'Just keep writing',was the response, 'and we'll tell you what you've done.' The writers weren't happy at all. The tendency of academics to treat writers as *idiots savants* who scribble away without knowing in the least what they're doing, has always been a source of tension, but this new wave of theory, which appeared to take the language of criticism totally out of the common domain, seemed something else again. Perversely, I became determined to find out what the post structuralists were talking about.

Despite the fact that I have made Doctor Swain the villain of this social satire, on a personal level I don't believe all his theory to be nonsense. Like all ideas that have impact, post structuralism would not have flourished if it did not have some insights to offer. There is no doubt that Nietzsche, the intellectual precursor of post structuralist throught, was onto something when he pointed out that humans find it very hard to be objective and rational. Most of us have been guilty of reconstructing our own history in a way that makes us the hero and the other party the villain and there have been many instances in which so- called historical, philosophical and scientific 'truths', have turned out to be heavily distorted. Power elites in every society have used the slipperiness of language to try and foist their 'constructed' version of the 'truth' on to minorities, but this doesn't mean that there is no *real* truth nor that literature is just another source of misinformation. While ideology can certainly be discerned in literature, it's not all that can be discerned. It is my belief, shared by the young protagonist of *Dead White Males*,

Angela Judd, that the great writers can still speak to us across the ages because they do offer us wisdom and insight about our common human nature.

Which brings me to Shakespeare. When I told my friend the academic Don Anderson, that I was thinking of satirising the excesses of the post structuralists, he alerted me to the controversy that had raged in the *London Review of Books* not long before. Called by the *LRB* 'Bardbiz' it had been initiated by Terrence Hawkes, a post structuralist professor of English at Cardiff University, who had declared that Shakespeare was a 'black hole' into which we fed our own needs and desires, and that his eminence in literature was not because of any special genius, but was due to the fact that his writings served conservative interests.

For the play, I decided that the central academic issue in Angela's mind would be over the literary status of Shakespeare and whether, in particular, his works were vehicles of sexist patriarchal ideology, a theory propounded by her lecturer, Dr Grant Swain.

I sent an outline off to my director Wayne Harrison. The story at this stage didn't include the physical presence of Shakespeare. Wayne rang me some days later and told me that while he was sitting in a theatre enduring 'an extremely boring play' he had had a vision of our play opening with Shakespeare being shot by Dr Swain. I raced to the word processor. With Shakespeare up there on stage, however, I thought it would be a pity to get rid of him immediately. We could kill him and still bring him back to defend himself, through Angela's consciousness, against the attacks of Doctor Swain.

Paradoxically, the inclusion of Shakespeare enabled me to take the play's concerns beyond the narrow focus of post structuralism and literary theory to the play's real concerns, the relationship between males and females in the last ten years of the twentieth century.

In the play, Shakespeare (who is not an attempt to recreate the real historical Shakespeare but is the Shakespeare Angela needs in order to make sense of her life), becomes a representative of his era, who believes that male and female natures are biologically different. Dr Swain, in contrast, believes culture is all-important and that biology plays no part. Angela is not sure, and to the end remains unsure, but in other areas of her life her certainty and wisdom grows.

Angela learns in unexpected ways when she adopts Doctor Swain's suggestion that she examine her family in order to discern its 'controlling ideologies'. She finds a grandfather who has behaved with a quiet heroism which belies his status as the chauvinist monster the family has 'constructed'; she finds a courageous mother wracked with guilt and exhaustion over the mother/career tug of war, and a father who loves both her and her mother, despite apparent layers of resentment. Angela, in short, finds that human nature *does* often break out of the strictures into which ideology tries to constrain it.

The play is partly a satire aimed at the political correctness enforced on society by the 'holy' ideologies of post structuralism, radical feminism and multiculturalism. The tone of the play is one of wryness rather than belligerent anger. It is an attempt to suggest to the adherents of those ideologies that they *are* ideologies and not 'truths', and that while ideologies typically contain truths they also contain untruths. It is not helpful to claim that all men are rapists or potential rapists. It is also, frankly, not true. It is also not true that all artistic products of minority groups are necessarily brilliant.It is also, surely, still faintly possible that heterosexual family life, despite its complications, can still be one interesting and valid way to live, and males and females are still capable of needing and loving each other.

I would like to thank Wayne Harrison, not just for the play's opening scene, but for his invaluable dramaturgical input during the play's development, and to Wayne, John Senczuk, Nick Schlieper, Tony David Cray, Tony Bartuccio, Marion Potts and the cast, John Howard, Michelle Doake, Henri Szeps, Anna Volska, Simon Chilvers, Patrick Dickson, Maggie Blinco, Kelly Butler, Glen Hazeldine, Barbara Stephens and Babs McMillan, for realising what I consider to be one of the finest productions I have ever been given in the Theatre.

Sydney, May 1995

The Text, the Actors and the Audience

Wayne Harrison

When David Williamson asked me to direct *Dead White Males* and
sent me a synopsis of the proposed play, I accepted the assignment
on the condition that I could use it to prove, once and for all, that
David was not a writer of pure naturalism. His work often has the
appearance of the everyday world, but his adventurousness with
structure, his heightened language and his selection of detail to
illustrate complex and tightly controlled thematics have always led
me to believe he is a great stylist. What I hoped to contribute was a
theatricality common to most of my work, a directorial style derived
from my admiration for the American musical – a very non-
naturalistic form – and Elizabethan popular theatre – a highly
imaginative, presentational form that had only three essential
elements: the text, the actors and the audience.

My role during the evolution of *Dead White Males* through eight
drafts was to urge David to manifest theatrically the highly artificial
nature of his writing, while at the same time preserving the
truthfulness of character and situation. My response to the central
proposition – a battle between new Australia and old Australia for
the heart, mind and body of the next generation – was to propose
opening with a short sharp image of the nightmarish extremity of
the battle:

'Mr Lennon?'

[*Pause*]

'Mr John Lennon?'

[*Bang*]

David ran with this idea, turning the fantasy into a function of
Angela's troubled conscience, and showing his true writing genius
by varying the uses of an embodied Shakespeare: as a defender of
liberal humansim; as a cognisant being, becoming aware of his

own shortcomings; as a suitor for the heart and mind of a girl capable of consigning him to the intellectual dustbin; and as an imagined surrogate for the grandfather the feminists in Angela's family had dismissed.

For a play that moves so fluidly between real and imagined worlds, I needed an open, fast, presentational stage much along Elizabethan lines. It seemed natural therefore, to draw on the results of the Elizabethan Experiment series, a ten-year research and development program I had shared with Dr. Philip Parsons, and which had explored Elizabethan performance conditions. *Dead White Males* designer John Senczuk had been a part of this series and indeed, had helped Philip and me carry the rough theatre style of our experiments (which had been usually performed in rehearsal rooms, warehouses and tents) into the Drama Theatre of the Sydney Opera House in 1992 with the Sydney Theatre Company's production of *Much Ado About Nothing*.

Put simply, this Opera House Elizabethan experiment placed actors, with a minimum of sets and properties, on a raked, highly presentational stage – a story-telling stage – and allowed them to join with the audience in the telling of the story of *Much Ado*. The stage we used in *Dead White Males* was almost an exact replica of the *Much Ado* set and was used in a remarkably similar fashion. To tell the story of *Dead White Males,* we used one chair, one tea trolley and a minimum of props, plus a band of adventurous actors talking to the audience. Their performances existed on an Elizabethan stage framed by a cool, slick proscenium arch suggestive of the university world of Dr. Swain: the old and the new in a scenic tension reinforced the thematics of the text. It was always Philip Parsons' hope that his persistent investigation into Elizabethan theatre would benefit contemporary Australian writers and their theatre, and the development process on *Dead White Males* was proof to us that the past could inform the present. The reaction to this first production has, if nothing else, shaken audience's perceptions of David Williamson's imaginary world, and put forward the proposition that our most successful adventurous contemporary playwright might also be one of our least naturalistic.

The Value of Literature

Keith Windschuttle

Anyone with the slightest interest in the theoretical issues dominating the faculties of arts and humanities today will find *Dead White Males* compelling. It is not only a very funny and revealing drama about personal relations at an Australian university, it is also a direct intervention in an intellectual debate. In many ways, it is the most daring play David Williamson has ever written.

In the past, Williamson has often drawn on the academic scene for a number of his characters and dramas. He has set two previous works on the campus itself. The 1974 play *The Department* laid bare the academic politics of one of the former colleges of advanced education. The film *Petersen* explored sexual liberation in the early 1970's university while making some acid observations about the elitism of English literary critics.

Dead White Males is also about literary critics but goes much further than departmental politics. It is a play about the value of literature itself and of the attempts by some people within the university system to destroy it.

The three central characters are Angela Judd, a young female student of English literature at 'New West University', Dr Grant Swain, her lecturer in literary theory, and William Shakespeare himself who comes back to life via Angela's imagination.

As you would expect from a Williamson play, it is located within an up-to-the-minute contemporary Australian setting with a cast of characters and a range of social issues that many of the audience will find excruciatingly identifiable. It is also a bitter satire on many of today's familiar poses of sexual and political rectitude.

Williamson's central concern is the purported 'Copernican revolution' that has taken place in the past decade within the humanities. This is the notion that French poststructuralist philosophy and literary theory have toppled the old certainties of Western culture. The canon of great works of the Western intellectual and literary tradition is no longer regarded as the expression of universal values but simply the out-of-date ideology of the dead white males of the Eurocentric capitalist patriarchy.

Williamson tackles this so-called 'paradigm shift' head-on through the works of Shakespeare, the penultimate author of the Western canon. He pits the wit of the bard against the literary theory of Grant Swain as the latter tries to indoctrinate and coerce his hapless students into accepting his own worldview.

From Swain's mouth streams forth all the theoreticist dogma that today's B.A. students are required to accept as gospel: there are no absolute truths; there is no fixed human nature; what we think of as reality is only an artifice; there are as many realities as there are ideologies or discourses which construct them; words don't simply mirror reality, they manufacture it.

Williamson portrays the current academic fashions with deadly accuracy. Swain regurgitates the lines of many of the leading gurus of theory. Quoting Michel Foucault, he argues that knowledge is always an effect of power and that liberal humanism is the principal ideology of the patriarchal corporate state. Echoing Edward Said, Swain claims the 'masterpieces' of Western literature have been complicit in enslaving blacks and people in the Third World. Following Roland Barthes, he tries to introduce his students to the notion of 'jouissance', a form of sexual enrapture unpolluted by the politics of gender.

This play will be especially revealing to all those students taking seminars this year on what is now the hottest topic in the humanities, 'the body'. While making a big show of his lofty non-sexist ideals, Swain reveals his interest in 'jouissance' and the bodies of his female students is much more than theoretical.

The funniest scene of the play comes from its assault on the pretensions of academic feminism. The Parisian theorist Helene Cixious has claimed women need a new language if they are to break out of an irretrievably male framework of thought. Williamson presents one female student attempting to pass her literary theory course through a hilarious Cixious-inspired attempt to subvert the dominant phallocentric discourse.

In the contest between Shakespeare and the odious Swain for Angela's mind, Williamson does load the dice in the bard's favour. He is a genuinely modest and delightful character who is most surprised to find his plays are still performed in the late 20th century.

In opposition to literary theory, Shakespeare argues there are some things that must be constant to human nature – the demons of love, grief, guilt, anger, fear, scorn, loyalty and hate. Moreover, he attempts to convince the audience that the two sexes have natures that differ in ways that go far deeper than ideology: they are born different.

Williamson weaves into his play some of the great scenes from Shakespeare's work including the wedding in the Forest of Arden that closes *As You Like It*. To incorporate extracts of Shakespeare into your own play is to take a huge theatrical risk. Handled badly, it could fall flat or, worse, look totally pretentious. Williamson, however, brings it off brilliantly. He does this partly because the scenes from Shakespeare fit so well into the movement of his own play but also because some of the Shakespearean scenes reverberate within the main sub-plot of his drama.

As well as a contest between Shakespeare and French theory, *Dead White Males* has a sub-plot about the impact of feminism on a typical suburban middle class family. Here again, Williamson taps into the reality of Australian life as it is being lived now.

Angela's father is one of the thousands of middle-aged male middle-management personnel who have been retrenched thanks to the recession we had to have. He knows he will never get another job. Her mother, on the other hand, is a successful corporate executive whose prospects have never been better.

Williamson's most moving treatment is reserved for Col Judd, the grandfather, a 77-year-old former building worker. The first time we meet him he sits impassively while his wife and three daughters berate him for being the authoritarian male chauvinist so familiar to readers of feminist analyses of the patriarchal family. Later, in a speech of great eloquence and power, Col tells the story of his life and defends himself from the charges earlier levelled at him.

When Shakespeare's characters come on stage to combat the literary theorists, Col appears as King Lear. This is a stunning moment for those who recall Col's previous two scenes and recognise what Williamson has accomplished. He has given the old Australian working class male – so reviled for the last twenty years by a younger generation of playwrights, comedians, and trendy theorists of all varieties – a theatrical apotheosis in the tragic figure of Lear.

For my money this is Williamson's most powerful play yet and also his most courageous. He is attacking a number of large, sacred cows including some, such as academic feminism, which are still revered by many among his long-faithful audience. Moreover, he is sticking his neck out and inviting the critics he is savaging to retaliate from the safety of their tenured chairs and lectureships.

At one stage in the play, Shakespeare tells the audience that he laid down his quill before he turned fifty and spent the last years of his life in deep melancholy. Williamson's fans will be glad that he has not followed the example. *Dead White Males* shows that, more than ever, he has the ability to identify important social and cultural issues and to say things about them that are both spot on and long overdue.

An edited version of this article appeared in the Higher Education Supplement of the *Australian*, 15 March 1995.

Was Shakespeare Really a Genius?

James Wood and Terence Hawkes

A new debate about Shakespeare has been sparked by an English academic who says he would rather watch *The Bill* on television than the Bard on stage. James Wood questioned Professor Terence Hawkes.

Terence Hawkes, Professor of English at the University of Wales, Cardiff, is one of the brightest exponents of a critical movement called cultural materialism. This school seeks to examine the uses we make of Shakespeare, and to lay all emphasis on the meaning with which we load Shakespeare, rather than on any meaning Shakespeare's plays might have themselves. Inevitably, this leads to questions of value: if we create Shakespeare, then how do we know if Shakespeare is any good? Why is Shakespeare any better as a writer than Cyril Tourneur? Professor Hawkes has likened Shakespeare to a black hole into which we throw our meanings, a writer of 'no necessary distinction'. Last year, he told the *Guardian* that he would rather watch *The Bill* on TV than go out to see Shakespeare, and that while jazz makes him dance for joy, Shakespeare does not.

James Wood: Professor Hawkes, in your new book, *King Lear* (published by Northcote House), you say that there has been much dispute over the years about whether *King Lear* is a 'masterpiece' and the logical extension to your position is that is may very well not be. But wouldn't you agree that even if we can't know if Lear is a masterpiece, the fact that we go back to it again and again suggests in itself some value.

Terence Hawkes: But I want to know who goes back and in what circumstances ... most people don't go home and take *King Lear* off the shelves; they watch TV. What directs people back to *King Lear* by and large is an education system which insists on having English at the core of its humanities program, and Shakespeare at the core of English.

JW: But using the critic Harold Bloom's definition of a canonical work, a 'strong' (or great) writer is one who exercises a powerful modification on other writers – so it's not just an academic-political institution that goes back again and again to Shakespeare, but writers recognise in their midst a strong precursor. Why do Goethe, Coleridge, Schlegel and so on turn to Shakespeare in particular?

TH: OK, it may well be that certain writers turn to other stronger writers, but it doesn't mean that any permanent value resides in such writers. Writers can be in the grip of prevailing orthodoxies and mythologies just like anyone else.

JW: The weakness of your position is that it leads you in the end practically to say, 'Shakespeare isn't any good.' You say that *King Lear* was not perceived as a masterpiece until the 20th century. But it isn't the case that *Lear* simply lay on the shelf between Nahum Tate's 1681 rewriting of it and World War ll.

TH: I think it practically is: there wasn't a performance of what we might call Shakespeare's *King Lear* probably until the 19th century; the Nahum Tate version was definitely performed. I'm not saying Shakespeare isn't any good, but what I'm saying is that the question of good isn't the business we're in. It's looking for things that are usable and thus are interesting and good for us to make our own culture out of.

JW: Well, that seems a very good definition to me of value: a text that is usable, interesting, valuable, even good for us. Why do we – in your terms – make use of certain texts again rather than others?

TH: You're going to say that we always use Shakespeare's plays. But it's very interesting to see which of Shakespeare's 30-odd plays are used at which times. *King Lear* doesn't come into the canon of great Shakespearean plays until the 20th century; in the 19th, the most interesting play was held to be *Hamlet* ... and so it goes. We use Shakespeare like this because he wrote this body of plays – they exist, and that's why we turn to them. Suppose Shakespeare had died at birth; would we be going around with a great hole in our culture? I don't think so. I think we would have turned to Marlowe or some other writer.

JW: Look, let's use your definition of value. It seems to me a perfectly good reason for discrimination between certain repositories of value – between certain works and certain writers. In other words, King Lear is a repository of useful value, and *Neighbours* isn't particularly. Yet certain critics perversely use your definition to suspend discrimination.

TH: Well, if you want to put it that way, I don't see anything wrong with it. I would certainly want to keep going back to Shakespeare because Shakespeare represents the ideological high ground. And if you abandon Shakespeare, then the education system will simply continue to make use of him, and we will have lost an opportunity to intervene in this making use of him. What I object to is saying that Shakespeare is a genius. We invent geniuses; they don't naturally occur.

JW: Let's turn to your idea that it is we who create meaning in Shakespeare. How much do we create? Clearly we don't invent the whole of Shakespeare, because then Shakespeare would simply resemble any other writer, and he doesn't. Furthermore, if we drain the text of all it generating properties, then we can't choose between rival readings of a play, and I'm accepting that you believe we can so choose. For instance, in the 1950's, in Czechoslovakia, the communist authorities made use of Shakespeare for their own ends. In productions of *Othello*, Iago was seen as an example of American capitalism, or simply fascism. If you were presented with that in a student's essay, you would disagree with it – not by appealing to other readings of the play (which is all you could do if you were following the logic of your black hole theory) but by appealing to the text.

TH: Yes, I would say, OK, show me where the language does this, and I'd guarantee the language never does simply this. But, like all texts, *Othello* doesn't say just one thing.

JW: But we have agreed that texts have properties – we don't simply create their meanings. We can then say that it might not be the case that we invest empty texts with our values and meanings, but that they come to us with their own values and meanings. The reason that I am pressing on this is because if texts have properties, those properties must be in part the products of an intending author.

TH: All texts have properties. They are not the product of an intending author but the product of the mechanism by which text is produced: writing. They are the product of having written language down which exposes certain characteristics of language ...

The other thing I disagree with is this vision of Shakespeare sitting in a garret, writing a pile of pages which slowly adds up to something called *Hamlet, Prince of Denmark*. We have never seen that manuscript. It doesn't exist. Furthermore, who wrote those texts? Is it Shakespeare, or is it one of the actors like Burbage? Shakespeare brings in his manuscript and Burbage says: 'This point where it says, "Shall or shall I not kill myself" – what if I say, "To be or not to be"?'

JW: But you don't create and shape those words and no amount of calibrating the extent to which we create the meanings in Shakespeare will alter this fact.

TH: Yeah, but the words are not in themselves beautiful. Take Leonte's words about the statue of Hermione in *The Winter's Tale* – 'oh she's warm.' One of the most overwhelming phrases in Shakespeare, but very ordinary words. What gives them impact is the context of the play. You say Shakespeare wrote these wonderful words; they are not wonderful words.

JW: I don't think that invalidates the notion of those words being put in our possession by an originating consciousness. Look, you are very fond, as I know, of Charmian's last words, 'Ah, soldier.' (Which, as you admit, was used by Eliot to demonstrate Shakespeare's superiority over Dryden's version.) There is something beautiful about the arrangement of those words.

TH: 'Ah, oh' – they are not words, they are almost pre-verbal aural sounds.

JW: You have agreed to being overwhelmed by Shakespeare and have agreed that we use Shakespeare more than most texts. It seems to me perverse that with all this you are so wary of ascribing to Shakespeare's texts a value and worth and to say,

'Yes, Shakespeare is a great poet.'

TH: You are like King Lear asking his daughters how much they love him, and I am like Cordelia who answers, 'Nothing' and then, 'according to my bond'. I don't want to allow historicism its full play. I believe in change in societies and the idea that certain texts are the products of genius freezes change, because it appeals to a notion of transcendent values. I don't believe in that. Who knows, another writer might come along who changes our idea of greatness.

This interview first published in the Guardian, *London and subsequently in the* Sydney Morning Herald *21 March 1995 and is published with kind permission of the* Guardian.

Dead White Males was first performed by the Sydney Theatre Company at the Drama Theatre, Sydney Opera House, 9 March 1995 with the following cast:

Michelle Doake	ANGELA JUDD
Patrick Dickson	WILLIAM SHAKESPEARE
John Howard	GRANT SWAIN
Kelly Butler	MELISSA
Glenn Hazeldine	STEVE
Simon Chilvers	COL JUDD
Maggie Blinco	GRACE JUDD
Henri Szeps	MARTIN JUDD
Anna Volska	SARAH JUDD
Barbara Stephens	JESSICA SQUIRES
Babs McMillan	MONICA JUDD

Directed by Wayne Harrison
Designed by John Senczuk
Lighting Design by Nick Schlieper
Assistant Director, Marion Potts
Composer, Tony David Cray
Choreographed by Tony Bartuccio

CHARACTERS

ANGELA JUDD, 19, a university student
WILLIAM SHAKESPEARE
GRANT SWAIN, a university lecturer
MELISSA, 19, Angela's friend and fellow student
STEVE, a student
COL JUDD, 77, Angela's grandfather
GRACE JUDD, 74, Angela's grandmother
MARTIN JUDD, 48, Angela's father
SARAH JUDD, 46, Angela's mother
JESSICA SQUIRES, 46, Angela's aunt
MONICA JUDD, 44, Angela's aunt

SETTING

The action takes place on the campus of New West University and in the Judd home.

ACT ONE

ANGELA'S ROOM

ANGELA JUDD, *an engaging young woman with a sharp mind, sits reading a volume of Shakespeare's plays. She looks up.* WILLIAM SHAKESPEARE *materialises, looking around him, puzzled at the modernity of the furnishings.* ANGELA *walks up to him nervously.*

ANGELA   Mr Shakespeare?

[SHAKESPEARE *looks up and smiles.*]

I hope I'm not interrupting, but I just felt I had to say – how much I admire your work.

SHAKES   I thank you.

ANGELA   How is it that you know – so much about us?

[SHAKESPEARE *is just about to answer when a* MAN *in his thirties, dressed in fashionable casual clothes, appears behind him.*]

MAN   He doesn't you know.

[*The* MAN *pulls out a pistol and shoots* SHAKESPEARE *dead.* ANGELA *looks at the* MAN, *horrified.*]

MAN   [*smiling*] Hi.

ANGELA   Why did you do that?

MAN   These are exciting times Angela. Dangerous and exciting times. You must know your enemies.

[*The* MAN *leaves.* ANGELA *is left staring at the body of* SHAKESPEARE.]

LECTURE THEATRE – NEW WEST UNIVERSITY

The MAN *who just shot* SHAKESPEARE *stands at a lectern smiling at us. He is charismatic, articulate and animated by the intense certainty that he has a supremely important message to communicate and that he is enormously well equipped to deliver it.*

SWAIN   My name is Dr Grant Swain. Welcome to the English and Cultural Studies Department and to my course, Literary Theory 1A. Most of you have always assumed that there are certain eternal 'truths' about 'human nature', that perceptive writers reveal to us. This course will show you that there are no absolute 'truths', that there is no fixed 'human nature' and that what we think of as 'reality' is always and only a manufactured reality. There are in fact as many 'realities' out there as there are *ideologies* which construct them. Christian ideology constructs a 'reality' which includes a gentleman called God ticking off your good deeds and your bad. Conservative ideology constructs a 'reality' which includes the belief that most humans are inherently dishonest and lazy. As a prerequisite to entry to this course I asked you to write a short paragraph on what you regard as the essential 'thinking' you. I have selected one of these to read to you.

[SWAIN *takes a sheet of paper in his hands and reads.*]

'I am sceptical of all ideologies, and try to weigh all the available evidence in order to make informed choices.' Would you indicate if you wrote that passage or wrote something that contained significant elements of that passage?

[SWAIN *notes the hands.*]

A lot of you. That statement, in fact, was written by me. It sounds as if it is a credo that warns against ideology, but in fact it is the defining statement of liberal humanism, one of the most powerful ideologies to have ever appeared in Western thought, liberal humanism. Liberal humanism, pictures you, the individual, as rational and free. Free to make your own choices. Free to control your lives.

But the fact is none of us are free, or can ever be, free of ideology. All of us are conditioned by inbuilt and often unconscious mind sets to act in certain predictable ways. Our life scripts, in fact, are written for us. By whom?

[SWAIN *looks closely at his audience.*]

Largely by legions of well paid 'experts' – economists, politicians, journalists and so on, who tell us the 'Truth' about 'The World', but it's not really 'Truth' we're being given, it's a series of ideological assertions. And the vast bulk of these assertions support the aims of the Western world's dominant ideology, the patriarchal corporate state. The project of patriarchal corporate ideology is simple. Keep corporate profits high and women in their place. Liberal humanism, in naively depicting us as capable of free and rational choice, is in fact the ideological handmaiden of the patriarchal corporate state. In encouraging us to believe we *are* in control of our lives it prevents us questioning the massive injustices to which most of us are subject. It is the aim of this course to show you how complicit the 'masterpieces' of liberal humanist literature have been in the process of depriving women, people of colour, people of non normative sexual orientation, and people of the non industrialised world, of power. The issues we will face go to the very heart of our understanding of ourselves and of the world. They are perhaps the most critical issues of our times.

OUTSIDE THE LECTURE THEATRE

ANGELA *talks to her friend* MELISSA DOHERTY, *who is extremely attractive, knows it and flaunts it.*

MELISSA   Do you believe any of that rubbish?

ANGELA   It made me think.

MELISSA   What? That you haven't got a free will, that you are totally manipulated by the evil patriarchy?

ANGELA   The patriarchy's real. My mother has to fight it every day. And I wrote that Liberal humanist credo almost word for word. I thought at first it was mine he read out.

[MELISSA *looks over her shoulder and turns excitedly back to* ANGELA.]

MELISSA   Those guys over there are talking about us.

[ANGELA *glances over her shoulder.*]

ANGELA   They're talking about you.

MELISSA   Don't always put yourself down Angela. You've got that fresh sort of beauty you don't need to spend time on.

ANGELA   How come *guys* don't seem to want to spend time on it either.

MELISSA   You look fine. It's just you scare them off.

ANGELA   How?

MELISSA   Frankly Angela, you're not good on signals of availability. Relax.

[ANGELA *looks over her shoulder again, more carefully this time. A particular young man,* STEVE, *who's not conventionally handsome but who is appealing in a run down sort of way, waves at her.* ANGELA *quickly looks away.*]

He's cute.

ANGELA   Melissa, he's *hopeless*.

MELISSA   He's cute.

ANGELA   Would you go out with him?

MELISSA   Aren't you interested in men at all?

ANGELA   Yes, but formed men, mature men, intelligent men.

MELISSA   Angela, even *I* can't get one like that. Come and we'll chat him up.

ANGELA   No, Melissa. No.

MELISSA   Check the body on that one.

ANGELA   The one picking his nose?

MELISSA   You'll never get anyone Angela.

DR SWAIN'S TUTORIAL

SWAIN, ANGELA, MELISSA *and* STEVE *are present and we assume a few others are too.*

MELISSA   But literature *must* contain truths about human nature, otherwise why would people bother reading it?

SWAIN   Because they *think* they *are* learning 'truths' about 'human nature', but all they're really getting is the version of 'human nature' that accords with the power interests of its author.

ANGELA   Literature has *no* wisdom to offer?

SWAIN   Literature is *never* about wisdom, Angela. At its base it is always about power. At base as Foucault, Althusser and Eagleton have shown us, all communication is ideological.

ANGELA   Surely we can step outside ideology?

SWAIN   Into what Angela?

STEVE   Reality.

SWAIN   Which particular version of reality Steve? Patriarchal ideology constructs a reality in which women can only feel normal if they're married and heterosexual, radical feminist ideology constructs a reality in which women can only feel normal as separatist lesbians.

MELISSA   No one 'constructs' my reality. I'm not becoming a lesbian and if I get married it'll be because I *choose* to be.

SWAIN   Your free liberal humanist autonomous self will make that choice?

MELISSA   Yes.

SWAIN   Why have you already ruled out the lesbian option?

MELISSA   Because I'm not attracted to women.

SWAIN   Could that possibly be because the dominant patriarchal ideology has constructed you to feel guilt and disgust at the very thought.

MELISSA   No one has 'constructed' me. I'm not a puppet!

SWAIN   Is it also possible that the dominant ideology has also constructed a female gender stereotype which includes words like 'emotional', 'tactful', 'unassertive', 'caring' and 'supportive', which it just so happens prepares females *extremely* well for heterosexual marriage.

ANGELA   Are you saying that all that's left for us is to choose our ideology?

SWAIN   Most people don't even have that luxury. They accept the dominant ideology as their 'reality'.

STEVE   By what criteria do you 'choose' an ideology?

SWAIN   On the basis of its social implications. I don't support radical feminism because its project is separatism, and I don't support the dominant ideology because its project privileges white middle class anglo celtic males.

ANGELA   Which ideology *do* you support?

SWAIN   My current subject position is non essentialist feminism and multiculturalism. Its project is the equal coexistence of us all.

COL AND GRACE JUDD'S LIVING ROOM

Three generations of the Judd family are gathered. ANGELA *is there together with her grandfather and grandmother* COL *and* GRACE JUDD, *her father and mother* MARTIN *and* SARAH JUDD, *her aunts,* JESSICA SQUIRES, *and* MONICA JUDD. *It is meant to be a birthday celebration for* COL*'s seventy-seventh birthday but, apart from a party hat that sits forlornly on* COL*'s head, there seems to be little in the way of celebration going on.* MONICA *has tears in her eyes.*

GRACE   Why did you ever believe him Monica?

JESSICA   Because she's a fool.

MONICA   He was going to leave her. He really was.

SARAH   Monica, I have to say that I think it's absolutely tragic that you spent eighteen years waiting around for a bastard who by the sound of it never had any intention of leaving his wife.

MONICA   He did.

SARAH   Twenty years ago you were on top of the world. I'd just got you reading Shulamith Firestone and you were starting to understand the feminist agenda, when you went and –

MONICA   I fell in love Sarah.

JESSICA   You're not a schoolgirl! If I ever hear one more woman, let alone my sister, say 'I fell in love,' as an excuse for some life wrecking piece of total insanity, I will vomit! Will you stop that wailing!

SARAH   Jessica, I know empathy is not one of your psychic priorities, but your sister is in some pain.

JESSICA   When has she ever *not* been in pain. I grew up with her. She pursues pain like a pig after truffles!

MONICA   You think I wanted this to happen?

JESSICA   Monica, anyone who wasn't deeply masochistic could have seen this disaster coming seventeen and three quarter years ago.

MONICA   Someone like you with a heart made out of nickel alloy might've, but some of us do fall in love!

JESSICA   Fine, then you had eighteen years of wild illicit passion, so think yourself lucky and *move on*!

MONICA   We aren't all emotionally equipped to dump our husbands and have a new lover every month like some people around here. [*Bitterly*] Pig after truffles.

JESSICA   It was just a figure of speech.

MONICA   Why that one?

JESSICA   Monica, it was just –

MONICA   Because I'm fat and ugly and I was lucky to hang onto

him for eighteen years, even as a part time mistress, eh?

JESSICA   I'm sorry. I chose the wrong figure of speech.

MONICA   You chose the one you meant to choose.

SARAH   Monica please don't torture yourself. You made a foolish mistake, but don't let it blight your life.

MARTIN   For God's sake.

SARAH   For God's sake, *what*!

MARTIN   If you're lonely and you need love you don't always make brilliant choices.

MONICA   Especially if you're fat and ugly!

MARTIN   I didn't mean that.

MONICA   Stop treating me as if I'm pathetic. I didn't come to Dad's birthday to be pitied!

SARAH   We don't pity you Monica. I just think it's sad that thirty years after the birth of the women's movement we are still allowing ourselves to believe that happiness requires us to have a man.

MARTIN   Sarah, the women's movement surely hasn't altered the fact that men need women and women need men.

SARAH   The one thing the women's movement has established beyond doubt is that *men* need women, but women certainly don't need *men*.

MARTIN   Excuse me while I slip out and kill myself.

SARAH   Don't be so defensive. I wasn't talking about us.

MARTIN   Oh great.

SARAH   I was talking about men who still cling to patriarchal attitudes. You don't.

MARTIN   No, I'm a certified wimp.

SARAH   You're as near as a male can be to non sexist, and given your background I think that's something you can be very proud of.

[SARAH *looks pointedly at* COL. GRACE *catches the look and reinforces it with her own glare of disapproval at her husband.*]

GRACE Ran this house as if he was bloody King Kong, and tried to teach Martin exactly the same habits.

[COL *looks at his wife, but says nothing.*]

Nothing but a bloody bully. I was the best saleswoman in Haberdashery in David Jones before the kids came along and Maggie Shortland wanted me to start up a shop with her but Boss Cocky here said no. She asked Carol Sheedy and the two of them made a fortune. We could've been rich instead of ending our life in this bloody dump.

[*She glares at* COL. COL *says nothing.*]

All it would have needed was a ten thousand investment and we would've been rich. And the headmistress at Randwick said Monica and Jessica *both* should have gone on to University but His Holiness here said no. Martin had gone and that was all we could afford. Where did all the money he earn go, that's what I'd like to know? On the bloody horses?

[*She glares at him.* COL *says nothing.* GRACE *turns to* ANGELA.]

When you get married Angela, make sure it's not a bully like your Grandfather.

SARAH I think marriage is the last thing on Angela's agenda Grace.

JESSICA Good.

SARAH A young woman these days would be crazy to even contemplate it.

MARTIN   Why?

SARAH   *Why?*

MARTIN   Sorry, but it's not quite so self evident to me as it is to you.

SARAH   Because unless she's unusually lucky, the best she can hope for is a man who will expect her to work full time, *and* to function as a concubine and housekeeper and whose skills of communication will be such that she'd be better off sharing her life with a Golden Retriever.

MARTIN   Thank you dear.

SARAH   Martin, I'm not *talking* about you. Will you please stop taking it so personally.

MARTIN   It's just a tiny bit hard not to, dearest.

SARAH   You went and did something about yourself.

GRACE   What?

MARTIN   Sarah.

            [MARTIN *looks at his father, embarrassed.* SARAH *catches the look.*]

SARAH   You don't have to be embarrassed. You should be proud.

MARTIN   I just don't –

SARAH   It saved our marriage. Why don't you tell your father. Admit you had the courage to seek help.

MARTIN   I don't want to talk about it.

            [SARAH *turns to* COL.]

SARAH   Martin was in therapy for three years.

MARTIN   Sarah!

SARAH   And the therapist said that his total inability to express himself emotionally was directly related to ... [*Looks at*

COL] ... a deficit of paternal warmth.

[COL *says nothing.*]

MARTIN Sarah, will you just shut up! It's Dad's birthday.

GRACE It's a wonder Martin ever recovered. Even during his exams Clint Eastwood here had him up at five o'clock each morning loading wooden battens on his truck.

[GRACE *glares at* COL.]

The girls could get away with murder, but he worked Martin like a dog.

MARTIN He needed help.

GRACE He could've hired an assistant. He was just too mean.

MARTIN At least it taught me –

SARAH It taught you that powerful males think they have a right to dominate and control and that young males think they have to suffer in silence until it's their turn to dominate and control, but let's forget all that for a moment. It *is* Col's birthday.

[*They turn and look at* COL.]

MONICA You're not saying much Dad.

GRACE He's mad at Jessica about that article.

JESSICA What article?

GRACE That one in the *Wentworth Courier*.

JESSICA How I've discovered my aboriginality? He was the one who told me.

MARTIN In all fairness Jessica, it was a bit rich.

JESSICA [*points to* COL] Dad said that it was quite possible that there was – his own words – a 'touch of the tar' somewhere in the family tree.

MARTIN Possible. He used the word possible.

JESSICA   I looked at the photos of Ern and there's an expressive
           nobility in his eyes that's unmistakable. And I'll tell you
           something Martin, rather than reacting with the horror
           that you seem to be –

MARTIN   I am not reacting with horror. I am just –

JESSICA   I felt a surge of immense pride and suddenly understood
           why I was an artist and why this country's landscapes
           had always meant so much to me.

MARTIN   I'd welcome it too, if it was actually true.

JESSICA   For years and years I'd had this extraordinary feeling
           that the landscapes and rocks were sentient beings trying
           to speak to me.

MARTIN   They were. They were saying, 'Go paint somewhere
           else.'

           [ANGELA *cannot stop herself giggling.*]

JESSICA   You have no understanding of the creative process
           Martin and quite frankly it's what's screwed up your
           life.

MARTIN   Really?

JESSICA   Yes really. All of us – all of us – have got an inner core
           of creativity that must be expressed, and it's only when
           we let that creativity speak that we become fulfilled and
           whole.

MARTIN   Jessica, your creativity speaks, but no one listens.

JESSICA   You're so cynical Martin. You had a burning desire to
           write a novel and you –

MARTIN   No one could ever finish my short story and that was
           only five pages.

JESSICA   [*to* COL] Dad I think it's wonderful to have discovered
           that we all have a *real* connection to this country. I

can't understand why you're upset.

[COL *remains impassive.*]

MARTIN   Jessica, you've got blue eyes and blonde hair. You're about as aboriginal as Arnold Schwarzenegger!

SARAH   Why is this all so threatening to you Martin?

MARTIN   It's not. It's just not true.

MONICA   If it was I'd be proud too.

GRACE   He's a racist like his father.

MARTIN   I am not, and neither is Dad.

GRACE   Not much. Monica was all set to marry that lovely Greek boy – what was his name Mon?

MONICA   [*new tears at the thought*] Spiros.

GRACE   Lovely boy. Monica and he were head over heels in love.

MONICA   Spiros Spyrokakadakis.

ANGELA   What happened Aunt Mon?

GRACE   Col was just *so* rude to him.

ANGELA   What did he say?

MONICA   'Are you an Australian citizen?'

GRACE   'If you aren't, don't come back until you are.'

ANGELA   [*shocked*] Grandpa!

[COL *remains impassive.*]

GRACE   Do you know what Angela? Spiros went on to found the biggest fruit juice company in the country.

MONICA   True Blue Juice.

GRACE   He bought a house in Point Piper for –

MONICA   Seven point two million. Three years ago.

GRACE   Hated migrants, hated aboriginals, hated anyone who wasn't fifth generation Australian like he was.

ANGELA   Grandpa that's so sad.

GRACE   Bloody old bigot.

ANGELA   Grandpa Australia's multicultural policy has been a *huge* success story. We've become the International showpiece of ethnic harmony. Other countries send delegations here to try and work out how we did it.

MARTIN   Total apathy.

GRACE   Don't waste your breath on them Angela.

JESSICA   Frankly, if this country was still full of people like father, I'd be elsewhere.

MARTIN   Jessica, it's his birthday.

JESSICA   I've decided it's about time I said something about that too. Every year, religiously, we all gather for this ritual celebration of *father's* birthday, while *mother*, who did the vast bulk of the hard work of bringing us up, gets a card or a phone call.

GRACE   If I'm lucky.

SARAH   I'm only an in-law so I've kept my peace, but I'm so glad it's been brought up, because it's been annoying me for years. In fact it's seemed to me very symbolic of the way things are in the Judd family.

MONICA   Exactly. Why should we all gather round every year and kiss his feet.

MARTIN   I haven't noticed too much leather licking here today.

SARAH   I just think it might be appropriate if we made it Grace's turn next year.

GRACE   I don't want that. You know how he'd react.

SARAH   Quite frankly I don't care how he reacts.

GRACE   I don't blame you, the way he tried to get rid of you.

SARAH   Let's not go into that.

ANGELA   What did he do, Mum?

SARAH   Just let's say it backfired. It only made me more determined to marry your father.

MARTIN   Happy day.

ANGELA   What did he do?

SARAH   He took me aside while your father was playing cricket or football or something and told me to stop wearing the pants – or go and find someone who had enough guts not to let me.

            [MARTIN *stares at his father, who says nothing.*]

            As far as I'm concerned we celebrate Grace's birthday next year or we celebrate none at all.

            [*There is a silence. They look at* COL.]

COL   No problem. This is going to be my last birthday in any case.

ANGELA'S ROOM

SHAKESPEARE *appears.* ANGELA *enters.*

ANGELA   Do you realise you're probably the most famous person in the history of the world?

SHAKES   [*stares at her*] But what of Beaumont and Fletcher?

ANGELA   No one's ever heard of them these days.

SHAKES   But t'was said by all they had more pithy and effectual

wit than I. They were noblemen.

ANGELA   Gone. Vanished.

SHAKES   Thou dost amaze me. In all the world's history *I* am of
              such import?

              [ANGELA *nods at him.*]

              I laid down this quill ere I turned fifty – its scribblings
              no longer garnered profit nor praise. My final years
              were spent in deepest melancholy, thinking that my life
              had been for nought.

ANGELA   It was all worth it.

              [ANGELA *hands him a bound volume of his collected
              works.* SHAKESPEARE *looks at it with amazement and
              begins thumbing through it.* SWAIN *comes up behind*
              SHAKESPEARE *with a pistol in his hand.*]

              Leave him!

              [SWAIN *shrugs and puts the pistol away, but wrenches
              the volume out of* SHAKESPEARE *'s hands.*]

SWAIN   He's a dead man in any case.

TUTORIAL ROOM

SWAIN *'s tutorial group is gathered.* SWAIN *places* SHAKESPEARE *'s
collected works disdainfully on the ground.*

SWAIN   Twenty, even ten years ago, you would have been here
              studying 'Literature' with a capital 'L'. By some
              mysterious process a 'Canon' of the great works of
              'Literature' would have been selected for you to study.
              These works would almost always be works by dead

white European males. The doyen of all of them of course would have been William Shakespeare. You would have been told that within this great literature those eternal 'truths' about 'human nature' were waiting to be found.

[*Silence.* SWAIN *waits a second or two.*]

All right. It's twenty years ago and we're reading Proust. He describes how if the Swann family received a visit, an invitation or even a mere friendly word from someone important, they would publicise this by any means at their disposal. We would decide that this social climbing tendency *was* part of 'Human nature', and taking our cue from the ironically disapproving tone of the narrator, a tendency not to be emulated. Our project of liberal humanist ethical self improvement would progress one step forward. Unfortunately the project was essentially dishonest and phoney.

STEVE   In what way?

SWAIN   In its assumption that 'Literature' *does* deliver penetrating and universal insights about 'human nature'.

MELISSA   Social climbing *is* surely part of human nature.

SWAIN   In some societies the loudest voices do hold sway, but there are many societies, like the Hopi Indians, in which social climbing is totally unknown. All a text ultimately contains are the ideologies a particular society has used to construct its social 'reality.'

ANGELA   Shakespeare's 'insights' into humanity are really just ideology?

SWAIN   Dressed up in the garb of brilliantly inventive metaphor and rhetoric, yes. Patriarchal ideology.

ANGELA   Then why is he the most famous person in the Earth's history?

SWAIN   Why is Madonna currently the second most famous?

Madonna used the metaphor and rhetoric of body language to suggest that she is the sexiest person alive, Shakespeare uses the metaphor and rhetoric of language to suggest that he is the wisest person who ever lived. My private feeling is that a night in bed with Madonna would reveal to me what a night in bed with Shakespeare has often revealed. Scratch the surface and there aint much goin' on underneath.

ANGELA   I'm not sure I can agree with that Dr Swain.

SWAIN   Let's all take Shakespeare to bed shall we and see if we can advance this debate a little further. And thank you all for being such a lively and questioning tutorial group.

OUTSIDE THE TUTORIAL ROOM

MELISSA   I told you we shouldn't've done this bloody unit Angela.

ANGELA   I'm finding it interesting.

MELISSA   You're joking. I'm going to see if I can switch to Professor Meacham's class. At least he still teaches *literature*, not this appalling 'theory'.

STEVE   They call Meacham the black hole. Go too near and time stands still.

MELISSA   Anything would be better than Swain.

          [MELISSA *sees someone out of the corner of her eye.*]

          Julian! Catch you two later.

          [*She moves off rapidly in full pursuit mode.*]

ANGELA   I'm not sure I agree with everything he says but *I* think the course is very stimulating.

STEVE   Really?

           [STEVE *looks depressed.*]

ANGELA   What's the matter?

STEVE   I can hardly understand a word he's saying. Does it
           really make sense to you? How can words 'construct'
           us?

ANGELA   It's just a fancy way of saying that we don't really have
           any truly original thoughts. Even the stuff we think of
           as our own ideas are really somebody else's.

STEVE   Is *that* all he's saying?

ANGELA   [*nods*] And because we think they're our very own
           thoughts we hardly ever question them.

STEVE   I shouldn't be here.

ANGELA   Where?

STEVE   At University. I had to do HSC twice and even then
           only got in by one mark.

ANGELA   Look, it –

STEVE   We both listen to Swain – I get brain fog, you get
           brilliant.

ANGELA   Not totally.

STEVE   Would you –

ANGELA   What?

STEVE   You like movies?

ANGELA   Some.

STEVE   Like to come to one?

ANGELA   Which one?

STEVE   Any one you like. I don't mind if it's a 'chick's' movie.

ANGELA   A 'Chick's' movie?

STEVE	Crying and stuff. I quite like 'em.
ANGELA	Steve –
STEVE	Wrong? Sexist?
ANGELA	Surely there aren't 'chicks' movies and 'guys' movies, there are just 'movies'.
STEVE	I read it in the paper. It said this is a full on 'chick's movie.'
ANGELA	That's exactly Dr Swain's point. The patriarchy would like us to think that males and females are essentially different but we don't have to believe it every time we read it.
STEVE	OK, lets see the Jean-Claude Van Damme flick.
ANGELA	No!
STEVE	Because it's a 'guy's' movie?
ANGELA	Because it depicts sexist and violent behavior as being natural and inevitable.
STEVE	All right, you choose the movie.
ANGELA	If we do go we should both choose.
STEVE	We can't choose a chick's movie, we can't choose a guy's movie? What the hell can we choose?
ANGELA	There *are* movies which depict women as intelligent –
STEVE	[*nodding*] Capable, courageous, calm, coping, resourceful, heroic, fantastic –
ANGELA	You prefer the sexist status quo?
STEVE	No! Look, I don't want to insult women, be unfair to women, patronise women, use women, or inhibit women, but every time I open my mouth I seem to do all five! I just want to know how to behave, because someday, believe it or not, I would like to live with a woman, maybe even – gasp – marry a woman. Would

you like to come to a movie or would you not? And that is *not* an implicit proposal of marriage *or* a signal of impending date rape.

ANGELA   Why are you asking me?

STEVE   [*swivelling around*] There's no one else around.

ANGELA   Seriously.

STEVE   Because I thought you might say yes.

ANGELA   Why didn't you ask Melissa?

STEVE   Do you think she would?

[ANGELA *is not amused.*]

You're more my type.

ANGELA   Why?

STEVE   Opposites attract. You're intelligent.

ANGELA   So's Melissa. She got a higher HSC score than I did.

STEVE   Have you got her number?

[ANGELA *is even less amused.*]

Why are you trying to push me onto Melissa? Every time I look at her she's got half a dozen guys around her that look as if they've been genetically engineered.

ANGELA   So you *are* asking me because you can't get her?

STEVE   Look, do you want to come to a movie or don't you?

ANGELA   I'll think about it.

[STEVE *shrugs and goes.* ANGELA *turns round to call him but he is gone. She admonishes herself.*]

ANGELA'S KITCHEN – HALF AN HOUR LATER

ANGELA *walks into her house in a foul mood.*

MARTIN   Angela, could you please unstack the dishwasher?

ANGELA   Do it yourself!

MARTIN   I'm cooking the meal for you and your mother!

ANGELA   I've got an *incredible* workload, I'm doing a subject called Lit Theory that is *extremely* demanding, but sure, I'll unstack the dishwasher, I'll take the rubbish out, I'll clean the bathroom. Who cares if I fail?

MARTIN   [*wearily*] Go and do your work. I'll do it.

ANGELA   And just tell Mum not to come up to my room and give me 'Agonies of the career woman part two thousand and ten.' I'm busy!

           [*She storms off.* MARTIN *stares after her.* SARAH *comes in.*]

SARAH   Angela home?

MARTIN   Yes.

SARAH   I'll just go upstairs and say hello to her.

MARTIN   I wouldn't.

SARAH   Why?

MARTIN   Our daughter is not currently in a parent-positive phase. How was life in the boardroom?

SARAH   It's always the same. I sit there listening in amazement as my rejected ideas come back, like the swallows to Capistrano, and are accepted instantly.

[*She tastes a spoonful of* MARTIN*'s cooking and tries to disguise the fact she is unimpressed.*]

We could have ordered take away. You didn't have to cook.

MARTIN   I quite like it. It fills in time. I'm still not in the Paul Bocuse class though am I, truthfully?

SARAH   I can truthfully say you are getting better.

[*She grins and kisses him affectionately on the cheek.*]

And you've always been stunning in the bedroom.

MARTIN   [*nods*] Not everyone can make a bed in under two minutes.

SARAH   [*pointing upstairs*] You're sure she wouldn't like –

MARTIN   Stay away. Believe me. Stay away.

[MARTIN *makes a sign of the cross to ward off the evil emanations coming from their daughter's room upstairs.*]

THE TUTORIAL ROOM

ANGELA *prepares to give her paper on* SHAKESPEARE.

ANGELA   I have to say that I started this essay with a great deal of scepticism. Because of this I deliberately chose one of Shakespeare's plays that I remembered as having a particularly vibrant and articulate female character who seemed to shape the agenda. I was certain that this play would absolutely refute the charge that Shakespeare wrote ideologically and from the perspective of the patriarchy. The play is *As You Like It* and the character is Rosalind.

[ANGELA *looks down at her paper and consults it intermittently from here on.*]

Rosalind flees her Uncle and goes to the Forest of Arden disguised as a man in order to protect herself. This allows her to test and tease her suitor Orlando, by warning him, in her guise as a man, of all the supposed frailties of womankind. Women, she tells him, are 'changeable, proud, capricious, apish, shallow, inconstant, full of tears, full of smiles, now liking him, now loathing him, now weeping for him, now spitting at him.' I got excited as I read it for surely Rosalind requires Orlando to disagree, but no, when Orlando reacts to this check list *approvingly* this is exactly the woman that Rosalind proceeds to *become*. She pines, she sighs, she gets paranoid he might run off with some other woman, gets distraught when he's late, faints when she hears he's been injured, and is so desperate to get married that she organises the wedding herself and tells Orlando, 'To you I give myself, for I am yours.' Patriarchal ideology has fashioned the characters, the values and the very structure of this play. Dr Swain's assertion that literature is essentially ideological couldn't in my opinion have been better illustrated.

STEVE   Hang on Angela.

ANGELA   Have you read the play Steve?

STEVE   Yes.

ANGELA   Is anything I've said untrue?

STEVE   No, but listen, the guy was writing four hundred years ago, and –

ANGELA   He was trapped within the values of his time, or perhaps cleverly and ironically sending up the values of his time?

STEVE   I guess.

ANGELA   At one point Rosalind apologises for interrupting her
             friend Celia but says she can't help it because she's a
             woman and women can't stop any thought they have
             coming straight out their mouths. Shakespeare isn't
             trapped in or *ironic* about patriarchal ideology, he's
             totally complicit, and in fact a major producer of that
             ideology.

MELISSA   Angela, don't be so humourless. Shakespeare's just
             having some fun.

ANGELA   Oh yes, the 'humourless' feminist. At whose *expense* is
             he having fun Melissa?

MELISSA   Don't get so worked up. All the literature these days is
             about what arseholes men are, so we're getting our own
             back.

ANGELA   Melissa, if you think the patriarchy has been overthrown
             because a few contemporary female writers are at last
             criticising it, then you're mistaken.

SWAIN   In general the patriarchy welcomes such criticism
             because it gives the appearance that change is underway
             when in fact the male monopoly on real power is still
             almost total.

             [ANGELA *exchanges a grateful look with* SWAIN.]

             Thank you for a most stimulating and incisive paper
             Angela. Could you perhaps give us a summary of your
             paper Melissa?

MELISSA   I looked at *The Taming of the Shrew*, because this is
             precisely where I expected to find ideology but I have
             to say I found little to none.

ANGELA   Melissa? You have to be joking. What about the
             relationship between Petruchio and Kate?

MELISSA   I think it's one of the sexiest I've ever read.

[ANGELA *is speechless with fury and disbelief.*]

ANGELA   Melissa, Petruchio does a deal with Kate's father to
          marry her for money –

MELISSA   Angela, –

ANGELA   Petruchio *announces* that Sunday is the wedding day, to
          which Kate says, quite rightly, 'I'll see thee hanged
          first,' and the next thing we know Kate turns up on
          Sunday and waits docilely for Petruchio to arrive. When
          he finally gets there he's wearing appalling clothes,
          drags her off before the start of her wedding reception,
          starves her, doesn't let her sleep and when she finally
          cracks after a period of prolonged psychological terror –

MELISSA   Angela –

ANGELA   She tells the other wives ...

          [ANGELA *picks up her copy of the text and flips to an
          obviously well marked passage.*]

          'Thy husband is thy Lord, thy life, thy keeper,
          Thy head, thy sovereign; one that cares for thee,
          And for thy maintenance; commits his body
          To painful labour both by sea and land,
          To watch the night in storms, the day in cold,
          Whilst thou liest warm at home, secure and safe;
          And craves no other tribute at thy hands
          But love, fair looks, and true obedience –
          Too little payment for so great a debt.'

MELISSA   Are you giving this paper or am I?

SWAIN   What's your reading then Melissa?

MELISSA   I think that Kate is spirited, sure, but also totally spoilt.

ANGELA   Oh Migod!

MELISSA   Angela!

SWAIN   Angela, let her have her say.

[ANGELA *fumes.*]

MELISSA   My reading is that Kate has been totally spoiled and indulged and that her undoubted intelligence has had no other outlet than to humiliate others. Petruchio is smart enough and tough enough to play her at her own game. He makes himself more bad tempered than she is to show her how others suffer from this kind of behaviour. He makes her for the first time in her life *empathise* with others. He changes her from a Shrew to a functioning human being.

ANGELA   So the super smart male triumphs over the moderately smart female upon which she declares him her Lord and Master and the natural patriarchal order is restored. Great.

MELISSA   That speech at the end is just lip service.

ANGELA   It's abject grovelling.

MELISSA   I bet that if Petruchio tried to pull anything two weeks after the play ends he'd get every bit as good as he got.

ANGELA   How can you assume that?

MELISSA   I just have a feeling.

STEVE   So do I.

ANGELA   You would. [*To* MELISSA] Why would Kate turn up to marry someone who's behaved like a pig to her?

MELISSA   Because she knows instinctively he's the only one who can tame her.

ANGELA   Spirited women need to find macho men to control them?

MELISSA   Maybe they do.

ANGELA   God, that says it all!

MELISSA   I'm sorry but I liked, was attracted to, and would probably marry someone like Petruchio. I am obviously a hopeless victim of the patriarchal construction of womanhood. I'm sorry. Shoot me.

SWAIN   Melissa, the whole point of this course is to allow you to identify the ideologies that are constraining you.

MELISSA I'm obviously trapped in and happily complicit with the dominant ideology. Just call me Bimbo brain.

[MELISSA *glares at* SWAIN *and* ANGELA *and leaves the tutorial.*]

OUTSIDE THE CLASS

ANGELA *is still fuming.*

STEVE   Hi.

ANGELA   Hi.

STEVE   Look, you had some good points but I think Melissa did too.

ANGELA   I'm sorry, but I think I was right.

STEVE   Fine. I suppose a film is out of the question?

ANGELA   Steve, I think this course *is* saying something important. Did you *really* think *Taming of the Shrew* wasn't sexist?

STEVE   Yes, *The Shrew* is definitely sexist. Husbands as Lords and Masters – definitely offensive to modern tastes.

ANGELA   And it doesn't worry you?

STEVE   Do you really think men are going to come surging out of a performance of *The Shrew*, bellowing, 'Back to the kitchen, bitch!' The ideology of feminism is beating the Bard hands down. Everywhere I *look* I see the humourless, sexually repressed, dour young women it's 'constructed'. They won't even go to movies.

ANGELA   I'm too busy.

STEVE   Does that mean no, not for the moment, or no, get lost for ever?

ANGELA   It means at the moment I'm busy.

STEVE   The thing I can't work out is how come babies are still apparently being born. It's obviously not going to happen much longer.

ANGELA   Ring up Melissa and act like Petruchio. You'll have all the babies you want.

                [ANGELA *turns and walks off angrily.*]

SWAIN'S OFFICE

ANGELA *is alone with* SWAIN.

ANGELA   It only takes a close look at the texts to show conclusively how conservative and patriarchal Shakespeare is. Why do people refuse to acknowledge it?

SWAIN   There's a huge Shakespeare industry worth billions of dollars Angela.

ANGELA   Why him? There were far better and more radical playwrights in his era like Marlowe and Webster and Middleton.

SWAIN   If the patriarchy is going to turn a writer into a profitable industry, the last thing they want is a radical. Shakespeare's great virtue is that he *is* so conservative.

'Usurpers' always get their just deserts, 'legitimate' authority triumphs, and the patriarchal hierarchy is preserved.

ANGELA   It's depressing.

SWAIN   Deeply. I warned you that this course might prove disturbing.

ANGELA   No, it's proved *enlightening*. I'm very glad I'm doing it.

SWAIN   Your marks reflect your enthusiasm. You're doing extremely well.

ANGELA   Thank you.

SWAIN   Thank *you*. It's a great feeling for me when bright students like yourself start to question received wisdom and think for themselves.

ANGELA   I just can't *believe* Melissa. We used to be good friends.

SWAIN   Yes, she is a worry. Her marks unfortunately reflect her lack of intellectual penetration.

ANGELA   She's not doing ...?

SWAIN   She's doing very badly.

ANGELA   I'm sorry to hear that. I think part of her trouble is that she still seems to totally define herself in terms of her attractiveness to men.

SWAIN   Sad.

ANGELA   In a sense I'm more sympathetic with Steve.

SWAIN   Why?

ANGELA   He's a man.

SWAIN   Being biologically male doesn't mean we have to adopt the repressive gender constructions of that role.

ANGELA   No of course.

SWAIN   Have you had any thoughts about your major

assignment?

ANGELA   No, I've been wracking my brains, but so far, nothing. That's actually why I'm here. To see if you could point me in possible directions.

SWAIN   I'm happy to suggest possibilities as long as you understand that they are only suggestions.

ANGELA   Of course.

SWAIN   Last year one of my best students did an analysis of the controlling ideologies operating within her family.

[ANGELA *looks at* SWAIN *with interest.*]

ANGELA   How interesting.

SWAIN   She found that every family member's history was totally incompatible with every other family member.

ANGELA   History is shaped in our own ideological self interests?

SWAIN   Exactly. Do you think your family might prove a fruitful site for an examination like that?

ANGELA   I think it could prove – extremely fruitful.

SWAIN   It's just a suggestion.

ANGELA   No, it's wonderful.

SWAIN   Don't feel bound –

ANGELA   No, it's a great idea. Dr Swain, –

SWAIN   Please call me Grant.

ANGELA   I just wanted to say ...

SWAIN   Go on.

ANGELA   Now I'm too embarrassed.

SWAIN   Go on.

ANGELA   When something enormously important happens in your life you should thank the person who helped you – I'm sorry – it's just so hard in this culture to –

SWAIN To what?

ANGELA To say simple things like 'thank you.'

SWAIN No need, I'm just doing my job.

ANGELA My mother's always been a red hot feminist, and I've always sort of believed I understood the issues, but it wasn't until I sat down and really looked at Shakespeare with newly critical eyes that I saw clearly and for the first time how *much* of our very being is manipulated and controlled by ideologies we're barely conscious of.

SWAIN I'm glad.

ANGELA I probably seem a very controlled and passionless person to you –

SWAIN Not at all –

ANGELA – but I have very, *very* strong feelings and I just felt as if the scales had suddenly been lifted from my eyes and I felt so *grateful* for what you'd done.

SWAIN It's my job.

ANGELA I know you're probably right and that we can never get outside ideology, but nevertheless I am so *happy* to be able to make the *choice* to step outside the narcissistic self centredness of liberal humanism and as a conscious *choice* join you in the constructivist feminist multiculturalist project.

SWAIN I'm very glad.

ANGELA It is *wonderful* to come into contact with someone who has a *genuine and non exploitative* concern for the interests of women and other exploited minorities.

SWAIN Thank you.

ANGELA I mean it.

SWAIN   Thank you, but in a sense it is just another form of selfishness.

ANGELA   How?

SWAIN   Like most of us who are at least part way human I am capable of feeling other's pain, and when I help alleviate some of that pain I am, in fact, relieving my own pain.

ANGELA   How come so many other white middle class males don't seem to feel minority pain like you do?

SWAIN   I have to admit, that *is* a mystery.

ANGELA   You're being too modest Grant.

SWAIN   No.

ANGELA   You are.

SWAIN   No.

ANGELA   The world out there is still full of Petruchios.

SWAIN   Surely less and less.

ANGELA   Don't believe it. They're everywhere.

SWAIN   How depressing.

ANGELA   I know I shouldn't tell you this, but if Petruchio walked into my bedroom tonight I'd spit on him, but if someone like you walked in – Oh God, now I'm going right over the top –

SWAIN   No, please –

ANGELA   I didn't mean it like that. I was just trying to say –

SWAIN   Of course, I understand totally.

ANGELA   Truly I wasn't trying to –

SWAIN   No, no of course not.

ANGELA   Now I'm just *so* embarrassed. I know you're a married man and I know that must have sounded like – it wasn't – truly it wasn't.

SWAIN You were expressing your feelings. That's fine. The whole point of the liberal humanist project is to constrain our behaviour within such tight ethical confines that we seldom express our feelings, and almost never act on them.

[ANGELA *looks at him.*]

ANGELA That's true isn't it?

SWAIN That's the whole point of the ideology.

[SWAIN *moves closer to her.*]

I have the same warm extremely warm feelings about you. Have you read Foucault?

ANGELA No.

SWAIN Foucault is mandatory reading in this area. He has established that Liberal humanism attempts to divert all focus off what Roland Barthe refers to as 'jouissance' and return it to the late Capitalist requirements of personal productive efficiency and endless consumerism.

ANGELA What exactly is 'Jouissance'?

SWAIN Like all signifiers there is no absolute closure on its meaning, but the approximate signifier would, I suppose, be 'joy of life', 'joy of simply being', 'spontaneity', 'joy in the free use of – one's body'.

[ANGELA *and* SWAIN *are by now very close.* ANGELA *backs off.*]

ANGELA Foucault. Which of his titles would you recommend?

SWAIN Angela, it should be obvious that I find you extremely attractive.

ANGELA Likewise, but ...

SWAIN   But?

ANGELA   But any sort of – liaison between –

SWAIN   Staff and students?

            [ANGELA *nods.*]

ANGELA   Raises all sorts of ethical issues.

SWAIN   All sorts of liberal humanist ethical issues.

ANGELA   Ah.

SWAIN   Foucault brilliantly exposes the way in which concepts of liberal humanist 'ethical responsibility' are used to prevent the expression of 'jouissance' in every structured organisation. Including Academia.

ANGELA   But you – you and your wife – there would be no shortage of – presumably – 'jouissance' in your lives.

SWAIN   Joanna accepted an appointment at James Cook University.

ANGELA   Queensland?

SWAIN   Associate Professor of Sociology. She's doing very well. Better than I am.

ANGELA   Ah.

SWAIN   Which makes me extremely proud of course. We try and see each other as much as possible.

ANGELA   I see.

SWAIN   But of course inevitably there's not as much – 'jouissance' between us as there used to be.

            [*He gives a hollowly nonchalant laugh.*]

            Do you like films?

ANGELA   Love them.

SWAIN   West African cuisine?

ANGELA   I've never actually –

SWAIN   Brilliant. Peasant fare without any trace of affectation.
           Are you free tonight?

ANGELA   [*tempted*] I'd like to but I've got a big history
           assignment.

SWAIN   Ah.

ANGELA   Five thousand words.

SWAIN   The Valhalla is showing *Godzilla Versus the Smog
           Monster*, which I'm told is an hilarious deconstruction
           of post war American foreign policy.

ANGELA   I think I'd better work on the essay.

SWAIN   When you've got a clear space?

ANGELA   I'd love to.

           [ANGELA *disengages herself reluctantly.*]

ANGELA'S ROOM

WILLIAM SHAKESPEARE *is sitting reading his collected works.*
ANGELA *comes in and listens to him before he realises she is there.*

SHAKES   To thine own self be true,
           And it must follow, as the night the day,
           Thou canst not then be false to any man.'

           [*He shakes his head in admiration.*]

           I can scarce believe I wrote it.

           [*He sees another.*]

           'There is nothing good or bad, but thinking makes it
           so.'

[*He shakes his head again. Then sees* ANGELA.]

ANGELA OK. Your language is exceptional. Inventive, musical, resonant.

SHAKES But?

ANGELA [*takes the book of quotations from him and reads*] 'There is a tide in the affairs of *men* / Which, taken at the flood leads on to fortune; / Omitted, all the voyage of their life / Is bound in shallows and in miseries.'

SHAKES [*nods*] A favorite of mine.

ANGELA Life's outcome is presented as only and always metaphorically subject to vast uncontrollable currents which must be exploited by a skilled *male* mariner at a single crucial instant in order to arrive at the privileged term 'fortune' in the fortune/failure dichotomy.

SHAKES [*puzzled*] Speakest thou English?

ANGELA William, there isn't just *one* instant of significant choice in our lives, –

SHAKES Had I stayed in Stratford and never seized the opportunity to become an actor –

ANGELA Then you would have been a far better husband to your wife and spared the world a succession of plays in which women are reduced to either ciphers or victims.

[SHAKESPEARE *stares at her.*]

SHAKES Marry, tis but a brief instance from thy happy disclosure that I am history's most favoured creation, to this new intelligence that I am soon t'be again its most obscure. And why? Some insufficiency in my *women*?

ANGELA See how you just said *women*. Like 'how could something as minor as *women* be my downfall.' Look I am sorry William, but there's a whole new agenda out there. It's hard to explain but your plays don't reflect the issues and realities of today.

SHAKES   But human nature is surely constant?

ANGELA   William you weren't really writing about human nature. You were writing your patriarchal *beliefs* about human nature.

SHAKES   Surely you jest?

ANGELA   [*shakes her head*] It's been definitively established by our leading thinkers that there is no fixed 'human nature'. We are infinitely malleable and act out the various roles imposed on us by the discourses and ideologies that construct us.

SHAKES   Pray tell me then which ideology has constructed the good Doctor Swain?

ANGELA   Like me, Dr Swain is committed to the project of feminist multiculturalism.

SHAKES   An ideology methinks which argues against the misuse of your sex?

ANGELA   That's its central proposition.

SHAKES   Then how is't the same Dr Swain did tempt thee with seduction's wiles?

ANGELA   No, sorry. That was *not* seduction William. That was an attempt to find 'jouissance'.

SHAKES   It seemed to me a sly conceit to lure thee to his bed.

ANGELA   Frankly William, that sort of remark is a good indication of why your writing *isn't* timeless. In future epochs men and women will find 'jouissance' in a non exploitative spirit of common consent.

[SHAKESPEARE *looks at her, a trace of a grin on his face.*]

SHAKES   Wilt thou then pursue 'jouissance' with the good Dr Swain?

ANGELA   Probably. I'd just like some time to think.

SHAKES   About what, I pray you? His choice of movies? *Godzilla Versus the Smog Monster?*

ANGELA   About emotional involvement.

SHAKES   But 'Jouissance', it doth seem, is pleasure without the irksome bonds of betrothal?

ANGELA   I haven't totally shaken myself free of the dominant ideology.

SHAKES   Could'st not thy hesitation issue rather from that 'human nature' thou claims thou hast not?

ANGELA   William, it's late. I need some sleep.

          [*She turns away.*]

SHAKES   Now is the summer of my new content
          Made deepest winter by that slimy sophist Swain.

ANGELA   Dr Swain has been courageous enough to point out that you misused your talent to help perpetuate female servitude. The ending of *As You Like It*, is an absolute disgrace.

SHAKES   'Tis surely one of the happiest most joyous endings of any play that I have wrought.

ANGELA   Not just *one* idealised wedding but *four*! Four female ciphers racing like lemmings towards total personality eclipse!

SHAKES   Eight human beings entering a joyous and fulfilling partnership!

ANGELA   Four women destroying themselves.

SHAKES   Have you ever seen it played?

ANGELA   I've read it.

SHAKES   T'was written to be played!

                  [SHAKESPEARE *gestures, the backdrop disappears, and suddenly we are in the Forest of Arden, and part way into the joyful marriage and reconciliation scene at the end of* As You Like It. COL *plays Duke Senior,* MELISSA *plays Rosalind,* STEVE *plays Orlando,* MARTIN *plays Touchstone,* SARAH *plays Audrey,* SWAIN *plays Oliver,* MONICA *plays Celia,* JESSICA *plays Hymen,* GRACE *plays Phebe, and* SHAKESPEARE *himself steps in at the last moment to play Silvius. Hymen, Rosalind and Celia enter to join the others. Sweet music plays.*]

JESSICA   Then is there mirth in heaven
                  When earthly things made even
                  Atone together.
                  Good Duke, receive thy daughter;
                  Hymen from heaven brought her,
                  Yea, brought her hither,
                  That thou mightst join her hand with his
                  Whose heart within his bosom is.

MELISSA   [*to* COL] To you I give myself, for I am yours.
                  [*To* STEVE] To you I give myself for I am yours.

COL   If there be truth in sight, you are my daughter.

STEVE   If there be truth in sight, you are my Rosalind.

                  [*Phebe sees that her hearthrob, Ganymede, has suddenly changed sex and become Rosalind.*]

GRACE   If sight and shape be true,
                  Why then my love adieu!

MELISSA   [*to* COL] I'll have no father, if you be not he.
                  [*To* STEVE] I'll have no husband if you be not he.
                  [*To* GRACE] Nor ne'er wed woman, if you be not she.

JESSICA   Peace ho! I bar confusion:
                  'Tis I must make conclusion
                  Of these most strange events.
                  Here's eight that must take hands

To join in Hymen's bands,
If truth holds true contents.

[*To* STEVE *and* MELISSA]

You and you no cross shall part.

[*To* SWAIN *and* MONICA]

You and you are heart in heart.

[*To* GRACE, *indicating* SHAKESPEARE]

You to his love must accord,
Or have a woman to your Lord.

[*To* MARTIN *and* SARAH]

You and you are sure together
As the winter to foul weather.

[*To all*]

Whiles a wedlock hymn we sing,
Feed yourselves with questioning,
That reason wonder may diminish
How thus we met, and these things finish.

[*The music swells and they all sing, hopefully in
brilliant harmony. During the chorus* JESSICA *leads*
ANGELA *across and sits her on* STEVE's *knee, ejecting*
MELISSA. ANGELA *finds herself participating in the
subsequent action.*]

ALL   Wedding is great Juno's crown,
               O blessed bond of board and bed!
               'Tis Hymen peoples every town;
               High wedlock then be honor·ed
               Honor, high honor, and renown
               To Hymen, god of every town!

STEVE   [*to* ANGELA] O my dear, welcome thou art to me.

ANGELA   [*to* STEVE] Now thou art mine;
               Thy faith my fancy to thee doth combine.

COL   Proceed, proceed. We will begin these rites,
           As we do trust they'll end, in true delights.

           [*The music rises and the newly weds execute a spirited
           and joyful nuptial dance.* SHAKESPEARE *notices* SWAIN
           edging towards ANGELA *and moves up to her.*]

SHAKES   Are things now so poorly twixt woman and man that
           you wish to banish even the *possibility* of a fruitful
           coupling?

SWAIN   Angela is intelligent enough to see this flossy tableaux
           for what it is. A hopelessly contrived and pernicious
           ideological confection aimed at perpetuating the
           patriarchy.

SHAKES   A fantastical, magical, diversion from the tepid
           weariness of sordid reality. A statement of hope.

SWAIN   [*drawing his pistol*] For four centuries we've suffered
           this insidious shit! Enough!

           [ANGELA *intervenes, placing herself angrily between the
           two men.*]

ANGELA   No!

           [SWAIN *reluctantly pockets his pistol.*]

SWAIN   [*to* ANGELA] What possible relevance has rubbish like
           that in a time when one in every two marriages ends in
           gut wrenching divorce!

SHAKES   [*to* ANGELA] What possible future is there for humanity
           without the bonding in love of woman and man!

           [ANGELA *looks from one to the other. She cannot
           choose. She clicks her fingers and* SHAKESPEARE *then*
           SWAIN *disappear. She looks worried and perplexed. She
           clicks her fingers again and she and the dance
           disappear as the lights snap off.*]

END OF ACT ONE

ACT TWO

LECTURE THEATRE

SWAIN *walks down towards his lectern.*

SWAIN   [*to audience*] Half way through the year I like to assemble you all again to talk about the sort of progress we are making in our various tutorial groups. The groups that I have been part of have proved very stimulating and from the reports I'm getting from my tutors I am getting the very definite impression that this is an unusually perceptive year. What is especially rewarding is how many of you are now starting to discern the sinews of manipulation underneath the cloak of ideological invisibility that the dominant ideology tries to draw about itself. The range and scope of the assignments you are about to commence is truly exciting. Nicky Yoh is investigating the rhetorical deceit used in a recent attempt to oppose a program of kindergarten cross dressing and non sexist play routines and Rosie Trundos is interrogating patriarchal assumptions in the rules of association of regional brass bands in the 1890's. One of the boldest investigations, is Angela Judd's proposal to look at the mythologies of her three generational family as controlling patriarchal texts, currently under interrogation by the contesting discourses of non essentialist feminism. I can't wait to grip Angela's – come to grips with Angela's – salient points in what I'm sure will be a precise anatomical – dissection of great position – precision. When you've started to collect your data Angela, please let's talk.

COL AND GRACE'S LIVING ROOM

ANGELA *is with her grandfather* COL. *She is fiddling with a tape recorder.* COL *watches her.*

COL   This is a University project?

ANGELA   [*nods*] How's your –

COL   Cancer? It's no big deal. My back's wrecked and I've been in more or less constant pain for the last forty years.

ANGELA   I'm sorry.

COL   Don't be. There's a time for all of us to go and I've reached it.

ANGELA   Everyone's going to be very sad.

COL   Come off it love. They'll all throw a bloody party.

ANGELA   I think that what they said at your birthday –

COL   You heard 'em. I've ruined all their bloody lives. What do you want me to talk about into that thing?

ANGELA   I just want you to answer some questions about how you see your life in retrospect.

COL   Retrospect's all I've got. So what are you trying to prove?

ANGELA   Nothing.

COL   Come on. You're a red hot feminist like your Mum aren't you?

ANGELA   I tend to see eye to eye with her on most things.

COL   So you're trying to show what a rotten old chauvinist bastard I've been aren't you?

ANGELA   I'm interested in how *you* see yourself.

COL   Do you think I ruined all their lives?

ANGELA   I'll be trying to keep as open a mind as possible.

COL   You'd be the first feminist that ever has.

ANGELA   Why do you say that?

COL   Well you're not interested in truth, none of you. You've just got a fixed set of ideas in your heads and the truth can go to hell.

ANGELA   There isn't an absolute 'truth' Grandpa, we socially construct 'truth', but look that's not –

COL   You lot have to have the babies. Much as you hate it, that's a truth and you're stuck with it.

ANGELA   We have the biological capacity to have babies, yes, but the *desire* to *have* babies is socially constructed, or at least intensified.

COL   Rubbish! It's in your bloody nature, and that's where all the trouble starts. If you're going to have your little bundle of joy you've got to find some idiot to start it and look after you. First choice naturally would be someone who looks like Mel Gibson and works as a heart surgeon, but you usually have to settle for choice number three hundred and ninety-six, so that poor coot cops it for the rest of his life because he's not Mel Gibson and he works as a roof tiler.

ANGELA   That's your explanation for the tension between the sexes?

COL   Yeah and I'm sticking with it.

ANGELA   Let's move on shall we? Is it true you advised my mother to stop her relationship with my father?

COL   Too right. And by Christ was I right about that one. Sorry, they're your parents, but if you try and tell me they're happy I'll laugh.

ANGELA   I think that basically they *are* happy.

COL   Are *you*?

ANGELA   I know Mum was away a lot, and I missed her, but I'm very proud of what she's achieved.

COL   You were bawling your eyes out the night you did so well in the school play. She was in bloody New York.

ANGELA   Yes I know, but –

COL   I saw you. I was there. She should have been bloody horsewhipped.

ANGELA   If Dad had had to be in New York you wouldn't have felt that.

COL   All right. I'm a dinosaur. I think mothers should be with their children. And you should have had one brother and sister at least. If you're going to have kids it's a crime just to have one.

ANGELA   Why?

COL   Only children get spoiled rotten and you're no exception. When's the last time you ever washed a dish?

ANGELA   It was Mum's choice not to have any more children and I can understand it. She was determined to have a career.

COL   What's so great about getting to the top in a firm that researches how to launch a new brand of cigarettes? Is that more important than being there when your daughter needs you? She ought to be horsewhipped!

ANGELA   Grandpa! You're being incredibly sexist!

COL   I'm telling you the truth as I see it! Ever since all that
            bra burning you think you can bully the Christ out of us
            and we've just got to sit here and take it.

ANGELA   Can't you see –

COL   I went to the bank yesterday and there's a woman teller
            with a sign behind her that says 'too many men, not
            enough bullets'. If the sign said 'too many women –'
            the guy would be hauled off to jail.

ANGELA   You've had the upper hand for eight thousand years –

COL   So now men cop it for the next eight thousand?

ANGELA   There's going to be a bit of evening up.

COL   A bit? It's the bloody duck hunting season and we're
            the ducks. Angela I'm too old to change the way I am,
            and I think you're a classy little heifer and that the
            world would have been better off with one more of you
            than one more cigarette brand. Let's leave it at that.

ANGELA   I think we'd better. You tried to get rid of my mother
            because you perceived her as being too strong?

COL   Is this confidential?

ANGELA   Absolutely.

COL   None of the family is ever going to read any of this?

ANGELA   I give you my word.

COL   It wasn't so much your mother being strong. Your
            father's too weak.

            [ANGELA *looks shocked and hurt.*]

            He's my son and I love him, but he's too nervy and
            anxious to please. Just about anyone can walk all over
            him. How's he coping since he lost his job?

ANGELA   Why haven't you asked him?

COL   I didn't want to embarrass him.

ANGELA   I think he would have appreciated it. I don't think he's adjusting very well.

COL   Poor kid. I knew he was in for a rough time right from the time he was four or five. He could never stand up for himself.

ANGELA   He didn't fit the traditional male role?

COL   If you can't stand up for yourself you sink, male or female. Jesus, you think your mother can't stand up for herself? The only difference between her and a pit bull terrier is that when *it's* going for the kill *its* jaws lock shut!

[ANGELA *ignores the insult.*]

ANGELA   Spiros Spyrokakadakis. Is it true that you –

COL   He wasn't serious about Monica.

ANGELA   Why do you say that?

COL   Have a close look at your Aunt. And she looked just as bad in those days.

[ANGELA *looks annoyed but controls herself.*]

Men get excited about women who look good. Sorry but no one 'constructs' that fact either.

[*Beat.*]

They've all got have someone to blame for the fact that their lives didn't pan out the way they'd dreamed and I'm it.

ANGELA   Monica and Jessica are bitter that they didn't get the chance to go to University.

COL   I know, they should have gone. They were both bright girls but things were really tough financially. They both should have gone.

ANGELA   Grandma says you were earning really good money and she still can't understand why things were so tight.

COL   You said you wanted to know how I view my life in retrospect? You really want to know?

ANGELA   Yes.

COL   OK. My life was tremendous, right up to the time I married your Grandmother. Cricket, football, billiards, dances, mates, motorbikes, the odd beer and a dead easy job – working for the council. Paradise. Then along comes this pretty little bit of fluff, butter wouldn't melt in her mouth, just wanted to please my every whim – hah, what a sucker I was. Suddenly – I'm married, but before I even get to find out what a tough little nut your Grandma really is, along comes the Second World War. So of course a bloke does the right thing and finds himself facing the invincible Imperial Japanese Army on the Kokoda trail. Now I'm not going to tell you what I went through up there, because I can hardly bear thinking about it even now. Most of my mates died, but I survived. Point one for your bloody feminist theories – when there's a war on and some poor fools have got to go it's blokes who get sent. And don't tell me it's the women who get raped because there wasn't any raping going on up there on the trail. All that was happening was that I was either delirious with malaria or getting shot at. OK, I get home from the war and the minute I climb into bed your Grandma is pregnant with your father. No pill in those days. She stops working and my council job is paid nowhere near enough for my new responsibilities. The only way to make enough money is to do some job that's so tough that not many others will do it. Like most of your sex you'll end up sitting on your bum somewhere working at a desk, so you'll never get to understand what it's like to lug millions of tiles up onto thousands of roofs, year in year out starting at five every morning. And when you're up there you know that one day, sooner or later, you're going to have your one bad fall. So you always take on a partner so you can help each other out with money when your time comes. I had my big one when I was in my early thirties. In hospital for three weeks but luckily, except for a back that was agony from there on in, I was more or less intact. The doctor said I should never have to go up on roofs again the back was so bad – three fused vertebrae – but by this time I had three kids.

ANGELA   Wasn't it about then that Grace wanted to go into business with her friend?

COL   No, that was later. I was offered a Greenkeeper's job which would've been easier on my back, but it didn't pay much and Grace didn't want to go back to work and leave the kids at that stage so back I went up on the roofs. Point two for you feminists. If a bloke has kids he's the one who finally has to earn the dough.

ANGELA   Not really. These days –

COL   It might be different these days but that's how it was then! Yeah now it's fine. You've got the pill and easy abortions, but in my day it wasn't so easy to plan. And in my day husbands didn't run out on their obligations. OK so I'm back up there on the roofs and every day is agony. Then disaster. My partner Billy Headen goes down twenty feet and he's finished for life. Total wreck. Now in those days there's no compensation, no insurance and I'm all Billy's got. He's saddled with three kids too, one of them six months old. Now the partnership is only meant to tide you over, but his wife could only get part time work and had to look after him as well as the kids.

ANGELA   You supported him?

COL   [*nods*] And this is the part your Grandmother's never known. I supported that family for nearly fifteen years. She knew I helped them out a bit but I never told her they got a third of what I earnt because I knew she would've screamed blue bloody murder. That's why we never had any cash to spare. That's why I couldn't find ten thousand to set her up in business. In any case her friends didn't make a fortune in that bloody dress shop. They barely made wages.

ANGELA   It seems a very – generous thing to have done for your friend.

COL   He would've done the same for me.

[ANGELA *looks at him.*]

So yeah, I gave your father a hard time, but I didn't have the money to pay an assistant. Someone had to help or I would've gone under.

[ANGELA *does not know what to say.*]

It makes me sick when I watch TV these days and it pushes the idea that life is happy and glamourous and easy. I'll tell you that for me and the majority of blokes in my generation life was anything but glamourous, it was sheer grinding bloody survival, and I'd just like the occasional woman somewhere, sometime to realise that and say 'thank you.'

ANGELA'S ROOM

ANGELA *is alone, thinking.* SHAKESPEARE *appears and sits down beside her. He holds up something he's been reading.*

SHAKES   I have read thy essay on *As You Like It*. And thy words on *The Taming of the Shrew*.

ANGELA   Did you understand what I was getting at?

SHAKES   [*reading*] 'Thy husband is thy Lord; thy life, thy keeper'
          – Somewhat in excess, I grant thee, but since meeting
          thy Grandfather this other should surely strike at thy
          heart.
          [*He reads*] 'One that cares for thee,
          And for thy maintenance; commits his body
          To painful labour both by sea and land,
          To watch the night in storms, the day in cold,
          Whilst thou liest warm at home, secure and safe;'
          He fought the –

ANGELA   Japanese.

SHAKES   Japanese. He bore score on score of tiles aloft to wintry
          roofs. And those [*He looks at her essay.*] 'idealised
          patriarchal alliances' thou disparage'st so – what of
          those fifteen years supporting his partner, sadly injured?

ANGELA   OK, it's a little more complicated than I thought, but
          don't try and tell me patriarchal power is a myth!

SHAKES   Thy grandfather did not seem to hold much of that
          patriarchal power. To me it doth seem to me he held
          absolutely none.

ANGELA   OK, some men don't have power, but at least they have
          the *chance* at power which is more than we ever get!

SHAKES   A woman of thy force of tongue will attain whatever
          she wants to attain. If you remain a 'victim' tis surely
          of your own doing.

          [ANGELA *looks at him.*]

ANGELA'S LIVING ROOM

ANGELA *is alone with her mother.*

SARAH   My life?

          [*Pause.*]

          Difficult.

ANGELA   Yes I can imagine.

SARAH   I'm not sure you can.

ANGELA   Of course I can't –

SARAH   Less than three percent of top management in this country are women. Did you know that?

ANGELA   You've told me. Often.

SARAH   You've heard me complaining, I know. But until you go through it yourself you really won't have any understanding. Do you know how guilty I felt about you?

ANGELA   I've told you. It's OK.

SARAH   Is it?

ANGELA   It's pretty obvious I'm not indelibly scarred.

SARAH   Is it?

ANGELA   Yes. And I'm proud of what you achieved.

SARAH   I'm still full of guilt. Up to here.

          [*She indicates a level above her head.*]

          Every time I see a movie with a mother cuddling her baby I get tears in my eyes. It's pathetic.

ANGELA   You were a good mother.

SARAH   I know I was probably fine. I was there on all the important occasions, but this society is so deeply sexist that it makes women in my position feel incredibly guilty. I know I was probably fine.

          [ANGELA *is silent.* SARAH *notes the silence.*]

I *was* there on every important occasion. Except that school play. And maybe a few others. I was fine. What's wrong? I wasn't there? Is that what you're saying?

ANGELA   I know how hard it was for you.

SARAH   I wasn't there? Is that what you're saying? Angela, you just don't know how hard it's been.

ANGELA   I know –

SARAH   When they found out I was pregnant all the men in that bloody firm practically cheered. They thought, hah, biology has caught up with the bitch. We won't see her around here for years. I'm not exaggerating. That's how they behaved. OK, you probably suffered a little, but I was determined that they were never going to be able to say that I couldn't cope with that job because ...

ANGELA   Of me.

SARAH   I was fighting for all women. And your father refused to pick up the slack. He wanted a child, desperate for one, but when you came you were suddenly *my* responsibility.

ANGELA   You didn't want a child?

SARAH   The timing could have been better. I was *glad* don't get me wrong, I was really *glad* when it happened, but the timing –

ANGELA   [*angry*] I'm sorry.

SARAH   Angela.

ANGELA   For being so inconvenient. I'm sorry.

SARAH   Angela as soon as I held you in my arms I knew I'd done the right thing. Believe me. And I loved nursing you. The only reason I went back to work so soon was that I wasn't going to give those bastards any ammunition to use against me.

ANGELA   Why was it so important?

SARAH   To succeed?

ANGELA   I mean it's not as if what you do is fantastically important to the future of the world. Launching a new soap powder.

[SARAH *stares at her.*]

SARAH   I see.

ANGELA   Look I know how hard it's been for you but at the end of the day –

SARAH   Why bother? Why not be a good mother to my child, then have another, then another? Because I wasn't going to let those bastards walk all over me. My mother was a pathetic meek squashed little creature who'd destroyed her brain with drink by the time she was fifty. There was no *way* I was ever going to be like that.

[SARAH *is close to tears but controls herself.*]

I'm sorry. I know you were hurt, but I can't be everything to everyone. I've got this *demon* inside me that won't allow me to let them win. I know you were hurt and it's still ripping me apart because you're the best thing that's ever happened in my life by far, which you might not believe, but it's true.

ANGELA   I believe it.

SARAH   Launching soap powders is not what I'm on about. I'm about showing that I can survive in their world and forcing them to respect me.

ANGELA   I know.

SARAH   I just made sure I was so competent, so bloody *competent* that they had to promote me. There are dozens of them and still only one of me and they still see me as some kind of threat.

ANGELA   Why?

SARAH   I'm a woman so I must want to change things. And of course I do. I want to get rid of all that macho posturing and introduce a management style that's sane and collaborative and inclusive but I haven't got a ghost of a chance. It takes all my energy just to survive. You've heard all this.

ANGELA   Go on, please.

SARAH   You want to know the truth? If your Dad had a job I'd resign. Ten years ago this job was the pinnacle I desperately aspired to, but now I just don't want to be a pioneer anymore. In twenty years time it might be better for women –

ANGELA   But surely you're helping make it better.

SARAH   Angela I'm battle weary. I just don't want to be in the front line. You can't ever be true to what you are.

ANGELA   Do you resent Dad for not having a job?

SARAH   Is it that obvious?

ANGELA   Sometimes.

SARAH   He could have held onto his job if he had have been a bit more confident and tenacious. He –

[SHAKESPEARE *appears behind* SARAH. *She can't see him but* ANGELA *can.*]

He – I don't know what I'm trying to say.

[*She pauses and then it strikes her.*]

You remember when we went to that production of *Taming of the Shrew* last year?

[ANGELA *nods apprehensively, looking at* SHAKESPEARE.]

I looked at Petruchio and said *yes!*

ANGELA   Mum!

SARAH   In fact I said *Yes, yes, yes!*

ANGELA   Mum!

SARAH   OK, your father's *lovely*. Everyone *likes* him, and I love him – but he's a bloody wimp!

[ANGELA *stares at her.*]

Angela, I read *The Female Eunuch* the day it was published and danced in the streets with joy. I've been a founding member of every women's group from W.E.L. to five different varieties of consciousness raising, and I taught assertiveness training on a voluntary basis for years, but if you want my honest advice, go find yourself someone with heaps of money, marry him and raise six kids!

ANGELA   Mum!

SARAH   It couldn't be a worse bloody life than I've had!

[SHAKESPEARE *nods at* ANGELA *who flicks her fingers and makes him disappear.*]

ANGELA'S KITCHEN

ANGELA *is interviewing her father.*

MARTIN   What did Dad and Mum say?

ANGELA   I promised them it was confidential. So is this.

[ANGELA *hesitates.*]

He's very guilty about how hard he worked you when you were young.

MARTIN   The funny part about that is that everyone assumes I
           hated it, including him, but nobody's bothered to ask
           me.

ANGELA   Didn't you?

MARTIN   Well it was bloody hard work, but I knew that he really
           did appreciate it. One day he even told me he
           couldn't've kept going without me, which is as close as
           Dad could ever get to expressing love.

ANGELA   Have you been all that much better?

           [MARTIN *looks at her with surprise.*]

           At expressing love?

MARTIN   You don't think I love you?

ANGELA   You didn't do all that much to show it.

MARTIN   Are you angry at me?

ANGELA   Yes, I guess I am.

MARTIN   Angela.

ANGELA   My most vivid memories of you are how irritated you
           were when you had to do anything for me.

MARTIN   I wasn't irritated at you. I was irritated at your mother.
           I know I shouldn't've been but I was.

ANGELA   And didn't you make it clear. 'You're mother's flitted
           off interstate again so I guess it's up to me.'

MARTIN   I might have said that once or twice.

ANGELA   You said it all the time. You gave her no support and
           you made me feel like a total burden.

MARTIN   I was the one that wanted a child.

ANGELA   Yes I know. Thank you father for my existence.

MARTIN   All right. I wasn't a totally reconstructed male. I did
           have this prejudice that a mother should look after her

child. At least as much as I did.

ANGELA   She did. In fact for all your irritation and your long sad sighs, she still did more than you did.

MARTIN   Women are naturally more nurturing than males.

ANGELA   Are they?

MARTIN   Yes. All except your mother.

ANGELA   Do you resent her success?

MARTIN   Yes.

ANGELA   Why?

MARTIN   Because I don't like being the failure of the family.

ANGELA   You're the one defining yourself as a failure.

MARTIN   You've just told me I've been a total failure as a father, and I was fired eighteen months ago and still haven't found another job. I don't think it's just a matter of how *I* define myself. The world seems to have passed a bit of a verdict as well.

ANGELA   You were never a failure as a father. I just had some criticism. And middle management positions have dried up all over the country. There are tens of thousands out of work like you.

MARTIN   You're mother's not. She's thriving.

ANGELA   You can't accept that Mum is the breadwinner?

MARTIN   I *accept* it. I take her money every week. I just find it demeaning.

ANGELA   Do you think you should?

MARTIN   I know I shouldn't but I do.

ANGELA   Do you realise what a strain that job is on her?

MARTIN   We hear it every night, don't we?

ANGELA   Do you realise that there's nothing she'd like better than to give it up?

[MARTIN *stares at her.*]

MARTIN   There's no way she'd give it up. It's her whole bloody life.

ANGELA   She's just about had as much as she can take.

MARTIN   Well that'd be lovely wouldn't it. *No* family income.

ANGELA   Couldn't you have held onto your job if you'd been a little more tenacious?

MARTIN   Is that what your mother said?

ANGELA   It's what I'm asking you.

MARTIN   Do you know why I lost my job? Because of that bloody therapy your mother made me do.

ANGELA   You've always blamed her for everything.

MARTIN   The general view around the firm during the takeover was that *I* was the one who had nothing to worry about. Then when the interview came I was stupid enough to tell them I'd done the therapy, thinking they'd be impressed.

ANGELA   They should have been.

MARTIN   You're joking. Male corporate culture has one strict rule. Never show weakness. Our team has got to always *seem* like winners to all those other corporate rivals out there. All that male 'kidding' and 'taking the piss' is just a male way of probing and testing to make sure there are no chinks in your armour.

ANGELA   I'm sure it wasn't the therapy.

MARTIN   They told me. It indicated I couldn't cope with stress. Out. So if I'm blaming your mother I've got good bloody reason.

ANGELA   If you're that resentful why have you stayed?

MARTIN   You want me out of here?

ANGELA   Dad, I didn't say that.

MARTIN   Why wouldn't you want me out? I've been no use to
            you. You said so yourself.

ANGELA   I didn't say that. There are just some things that really
            hurt me and after all these years I want you to know.

MARTIN   All right, I might have grumbled a bit, but I did take
            you to ballet, music, drama, sport, shopping for clothes,
            to movies, to parties –

ANGELA   Other girls Dad's ...

MARTIN   Other girls Dad's what?

ANGELA   They ... sometimes they ... compliment their daughters.
            Say how ... nice they look. Joke about how they'll have
            to keep an eye on all the boys ... you never ... you never
            once made me feel ... attractive.

MARTIN   [*stares at her, then explodes*] Your mother said that's
            what men shouldn't *do* anymore! Women don't want to
            hear that stuff. They want to be appreciated for their
            talents, their minds!

ANGELA   Did you ... ever? Think I was ...

MARTIN   Of course you are! How am I supposed to know that's
            what you want to hear when your mother –

ANGELA   Don't keep blaming Mum! Haven't you got a mind of
            your own! Sometimes couldn't you just act a bit more
            like a ...

MARTIN   Man? A man?

ANGELA   [*angrily*] Yes! Go out there and get a job! Thump on
            someone's desk until they give you one! Don't be such
            a bloody wimp!

[MARTIN *stares at her.* SHAKESPEARE *enters.*]

MARTIN   So this is the truth of it, is it? Women scream at us for being brutes and tell us to get sensitive and caring or they'll walk, but all the time they secretly want ...

[*He searches his memory banks.* SHAKESPEARE *knows what he's looking for and urges him on.*]

Petruchio!

[SHAKESPEARE *beams.* ANGELA *looks away.*]

Your mother came out of that production last year muttering about how sexist it was, but that's what you all bloody well want. Petruchio! Isn't it?

ANGELA   I don't know!

MARTIN   You know something? I don't want to thump on desks and get another job. When I was fired I was enormously angry but eighteen months on I'm starting to realise how much I hated it all. Never once in my career did I have any real autonomy. Someone was always looking over my shoulder and I hated it.

ANGELA   You're not even *trying* to get another job?

MARTIN   No. Not any more. After eighteen months of crawling on my belly to personnel managers I wouldn't have spat at five years ago I've had enough. I'm sorry your mother is finding the going hard, but I'm not Petruchio, so bad bloody luck the both of you!

[*He turns angrily and goes.* ANGELA *glares at* SHAKESPEARE *and flicks him out of existence again.*]

CAMPUS GROUNDS – NEXT DAY

STEVE *is sitting looking despondent.* MELISSA *walks up and sits beside him.*

MELISSA   Seen your assessment on the notice board? We're both going to fail.

STEVE   [*nods*] I've known that all along.

MELISSA   Seen darling little Angela's mark? A plus.

STEVE   Yeah.

MELISSA   It's disgusting. Suck up to Swain or fail.

STEVE   Yeah.

MELISSA   This isn't education, it's full on indoctrination. Join the post structuralist feminist multiculturalist project or fail.

STEVE   That's the message.

MELISSA   I'm so bloody furious. If I fail it effectively adds another year onto my course.

STEVE   This is going to be my last year in any case.

            [MELISSA *looks at him enquiringly.*]

            I'm failing all my subjects. It's all just words, words, words. I hate this place.

MELISSA   Why are you here?

STEVE   My father's an academic, my mother's an academic, and they can't believe that I'm not. You know what I really like doing? Fixing cars. I spent seven hours putting a mate's engine together last weekend and it was great. Not that I can tell *them* that.

MELISSA   Why not?

STEVE   They think that only slobs fix cars. And so do you and Angela.

MELISSA   Everyone should do what they like doing.

STEVE   Yeah, yeah.

MELISSA   Angela thinks you're really nice.

STEVE   She won't even go to a movie with me!

MELISSA   She's very – cautious about men.

STEVE   Cautious? Every time I meet her I feel like she's reading a sign on my forehead that says, 'Beware, contains testosterone.' Will it really add a year to your course?

MELISSA   [*nods*] There is no way I'm going to spend another year waitressing at the Waltzing Matilda Tavern.

STEVE   Grim?

MELISSA   How would you like to wear a sheepskin and hear Japanese tourists sing 'Click go the shears', four nights a week?

STEVE   More fun than pouring beers at the gayest pub in Sydney.

MELISSA   Do you get propositioned?

STEVE   No. Which sort of adds insult to injury.

MELISSA   I'm going to pass this bloody course Steve.

STEVE   Toe the ideological line?

MELISSA   Yep. Sorry. When I balance integrity against the Waltzing Matilda, the feminist multiculturalist project starts to make a lot of sense.

STEVE   You couldn't bring yourself to parrot that crap?

MELISSA   Watch me.

STEVE   What, you're just going to rock up to next class a convert?

MELISSA   No, no. You get much better marks if your teacher's arguments are so lucid and compelling that you have a full on, high voltage, conversion experience.

           [MELISSA *mimes listening carefully to* SWAIN *then suddenly the electric light bulb goes on above her head. She sees.* STEVE *laughs.*]

SWAIN *and* MELISSA *alone.*

MELISSA   I was just so shocked. I never done as badly as that before and I just wanted to see if there was anything I could do about it before it's too late.

SWAIN   I hate failing anyone Melissa, I really do, but the standard of your arguments has been quite – depressing.

MELISSA   I know I haven't been following the anti humanist line –

SWAIN   You're not required to follow any particular line, Melissa. This is an institution of tertiary study.

MELISSA   Yes, but –

SWAIN   It's simply that the arguments you mount in defense of your liberal humanist position are inadequate.

MELISSA   What sort of argument *would* be adequate?

SWAIN   I do have to say that working within your chosen framework makes adequate argument very very difficult.

MELISSA   [*pleading*] I just can't see *how* and *where* the dominant patriarchal corporate state pumps out this *incessant* message? You make it sound like there's a room somewhere where the patriarchy meet to decide how best to grind women into the dust.

SWAIN   No, no. The message is diffuse and comes from thousands of sources some of which aren't even conscious they're sending it.

MELISSA   Can you give me an *example* – a concrete *example*. I don't want to be stupid and naive, but I just don't *get* it!

SWAIN   OK. A TV ad I saw last night. A small boy comes home bruised, filthy and disconsolate because his football team has been defeated. Mother comforts him by washing his football gear sparkling clean with the aid of 'Surge' or 'Splurge', a 'breakthrough' miracle detergent. The ideological message? Young male warrior wounded in battle is nursed by maternal female who mends his armour and sends him back to the battlefield. Men fight, women nurture.

MELISSA   [*frowns*] And the advertising agency is in effect acting as an independent branch of Patriarchy limited?

SWAIN   [*nods*] No one *directs* them to. They just know that because most of the so called 'free' minds out there are in fact thoroughly brainwashed by corporate patriarchal ideology, they'll think the message is 'cute'. Men *are* warriors, women *are* nurturers, that's the way things are and always will be. That's 'reality'.

[MELISSA *stares at him and has a beautifully performed 'conversion' experience of great intensity.*]

MELISSA   Hey! Yeah! Yeah! You never see a grubby battered little girl come home and hand her tunic to Dad, do you?

SWAIN   Wouldn't sell.

MELISSA   [*sudden new insight*] Those breakfast food commercials – it's always the mother being nurturing and caring and the father being wise, knowing and – patriarchal.

SWAIN   Exactly.

MELISSA   So the patriarchal message comes from a thousand different throats in a thousand different guises?

SWAIN   Precisely.

MELISSA   Suddenly it all makes sense.

SWAIN   My fault. I should have given you some concrete examples.

MELISSA   No, no, no. My fault. I should have asked. Suddenly the

fog has lifted. [*New thought.*] Tell me, tell me. If the dominant ideology is so *dominant*, how do the oppositional ideologies get started?

SWAIN   Out of the lived experience of oppressed minorities.

MELISSA   Right, right. *Right!*

SWAIN   Oppressed minorities are the site of the generation of all that's vital and valuable in our culture.

MELISSA   Right! Oh MiGod. I came in here *totally* depressed and confused and in a few moments you turn that all around and now I can see *exactly* what's going on.

SWAIN   I should have given you some concrete examples earlier.

MELISSA   No, no. Please. What you did is *fantastic*. Is it still possible that if my major project is good I could pass Dr Swain?

SWAIN   Absolutely. And please, call me Grant. Have you chosen the topic?

MELISSA   No, I've been terrified, totally paralysed. Up to now my mind has been a total blank.

SWAIN   But you feel more confident now?

MELISSA   Indescribably more confident. It's just that I've lost so much time.

SWAIN   I'm sure I can help steer you in the right direction. Do you like West African food?

MELISSA   Absolutely adore it. Simple and totally unpretentious.

SWAIN   Exactly. How are you placed tonight?

MELISSA   Grant, the sooner the better.

CAMPUS – NEXT DAY

ANGELA *sees* SWAIN *and stops him.*

ANGELA   Grant, do you have a second?

SWAIN   Of course.

ANGELA   My assignment is turning out to be a little more – difficult to interpret than I thought.

SWAIN   Really?

ANGELA   I wondered if we could possibly talk about it.

SWAIN   Of course.

ANGELA   Grant, I feel really stupid about the dumb way I – you must have – I didn't have a history assignment – I'd love to have a West African meal.

SWAIN   Ah.

ANGELA   If you think that's an appropriate way to discuss the assignment.

SWAIN   Ah, Angela. I've been thinking this through a little more rigorously.

ANGELA   Oh?

SWAIN   Foucault is absolutely right of course. We are encouraged to deny ourselves spontaneity and 'jouissance' –

ANGELA   I've been reading him. The decentred self offers endless possibilities of intellectual and sensual 'play' –

SWAIN   Absolutely, but the political reality I didn't fully address, is that the head of faculty, Professor Meacham, is a fanatical liberal humanist who has the numbers on the University Council, and if I was to be discovered in any kind of intimate association with a student he'd play that tactical card against me for all it was worth.

ANGELA   Oh. Can I still see you about the assignment?

SWAIN   Of course. But not over a meal. The feminist multicultural project is too important to put at risk. I'm sorry Angela, I'm so embarrassed.

ANGELA   Please don't be. I wasn't at all sure I would've wanted anything more than the meal in any case. My main worry is about the assignment. The material is proving quite hard to analyse.

SWAIN   I'm absolutely sure it's going to be fine.

ANGELA   Can I extend the due date a little? I need more time to think.

SWAIN   Absolutely. I'll move Melissa's presentation forward and yours back. She seems to be making very good progress.

ANGELA   Melissa?

SWAIN   She seems to have overcome all that initial resistance and is becoming very committed.

[ANGELA *frowns.*]

THE TUTORIAL ROOM

MELISSA *prepares to deliver her paper.* SWAIN, STEVE *and* ANGELA *listen.*

MELISSA   The more I researched, the more obvious it became to me that the *real* artistic excitement in Western Society is coming from the originary ideological accretions occurring out of the lived experience of the disadvantaged groups currently contesting the traditional sites of the dominant discourse. Working on some leads kindly given to me by Dr Swain, I have encountered the work of the so far unpublished Geraldton feminist lesbian writer of ethnic Egyptian origin, Sophie Tsalis. Tsalis accepts Helene Cixous' position that language itself is saturated with patriarchal binary opposites such as male/female, mind/body, rational/intuitive, logical/emotive, which inevitably privilege the male term, thus making it impossible for women to communicate their 'reality' within this irretrievably male discourse. The project to which Cixous and Tsalis are committed is the creation of a new female language. I'd like to read you an extract which may give you some of the flavour of this exciting project, which Tsalis describes as a subversive intervention and interrogation of the phallocentric dominant discourse.

            [MELISSA *opens her book and reads.*]

            'You big. You ugly. You poor dick. You stupid dick. Why? Why? Why? Why you shout? Zweee. Zweeebub. You think you smart but you dumb. I smarter. Someday. Someday soon. Just wait. Zweee. Zweesome. Zweesee. Zweebub. Zweebub Vorgone. I smart. Just wait. Ziggly Zweebub, Ziggly Zukoff. No more Zukoff for you Zweebub. Sickly ickly dickly – Zukoff yourself. And swallow. No more swallow from Ziggly. No more nothing. Never.

STEVE   Melissa, that's crap!

SWAIN   It is if viewed from the dominant discourse.

STEVE   It's crap from any discourse.

SWAIN   When that piece was read to Sophie's group in

Geraldton the response was electric.

STEVE   Then they're all as stupid as she is.

SWAIN   You're saying that you're prepared to denigrate the responses of another group of people because they don't correspond to yours.

STEVE   In this case, yes. If they like listening to feminist nursery rhymes fine, but don't try and tell me it's a new language.

SWAIN   Steve, you can use rhetorical abuse to denigrate, but you will have to explain to me why Sophie's writing has far more power for significant numbers of people than *Hamlet* ever will.

STEVE   Because it's crudely ideological.

SWAIN   So is *Hamlet*.

ANGELA   Melissa, do you really believe that's good writing?

MELISSA   I believe it is effective writing for the purposes for which it was written. Like Grant I believe that there can never be absolute aesthetic standards. Judgement *always* depends on the ideological framework from which the work is viewed.

OUTSIDE THE TUTORIAL

ANGELA *and* STEVE *collar* MELISSA.

ANGELA   You're sleeping with him, aren't you?

MELISSA   Don't be ridiculous.

ANGELA   You are.

MELISSA   I can keep an idiot like that waiting around in hope for as long as I like. From what I hear *you* were the one who was all ready to jump straight into bed.

ANGELA   [*embarrassed in front of* STEVE] I was going to have a meal with him, that's all!

MELISSA   Oh yes. Sure.

ANGELA   And it was only because I thought he was a very special person.

MELISSA   He is. He decides who passes and who fails.

ANGELA   Melissa, you're vile.

MELISSA   Power is the only reality. Read your Foucault.

ANGELA   You don't believe a word of that crap you just gave us in the tutorial.

MELISSA   You can afford your principles Angela. You don't have to work four nights a week at the Waltzing Matilda.

            [MELISSA *walks off.* ANGELA *looks embarrassed as she looks at* STEVE.]

ANGELA   I was just going to have a meal with him. To discuss my project.

            [STEVE *nods.*]

            OK. I was – I thought – I thought he *was* something special.

STEVE   He's an arsehole!

ANGELA   I still think there is *some* truth in what he says.

STEVE   You were prepared to sleep with him, yet you won't even come out to a *movie* with me!

ANGELA   I'm sorry. We'll go to a movie.

STEVE   Forget it!

            [STEVE *storms off.* ANGELA *looks disconsolate.*]

ANGELA'S ROOM

SHAKESPEARE *is sitting on the floor with a large pile of books beside him. He is looking exhausted.* ANGELA *enters looking fired up and purposeful.*

ANGELA   I need some answers William.

SHAKES   [*indicating books*] You will not find them here.

ANGELA   What are you reading?

SHAKES   All those vile 'feminist' books that are thy mothers and all those viler 'literary theory' books of thine.

ANGELA   They're new ways of thinking –

SHAKES   That prattling knave Swain speaks through his fundament. Of course there is a human nature, and that of man and woman surely differs.

ANGELA   William –

SHAKES   Man is a prancing cockerel. Arrogant, proud, like Petruchio.

ANGELA   My father is no Petruchio and my mother fights to the death.

SHAKES   Every man who is not Petruchio doth wish he was, and every woman who is a Shrew doth wish she was not.

ANGELA   Only because of our conditioning!

SHAKES   Two natures as divers as man and woman cannot be forced identical. [*He holds up one of the feminist books.*] 'Tis in this present putrid project that misery is spawned.

ANGELA   You *are* deeply conservative William. Deeply, deeply conservative.

SHAKES   Make such gains as are just, but beyond a certain point the war will wither both sexes, for men are bred for battle and fight beyond all semblance of reason.

ANGELA   William if you breathed a word of that reactionary essentialist drivel to some women I know you'd be ripped apart.

SHAKES   [*he holds up a feminist book*] Since reading thy mother's books I am sure thou art right. [*He throws the book away.*] Right glad I am to have lived in mine own time.

ANGELA   Give me one piece of evidence to support what you're saying –

SHAKES   What hath caused all history to be littered with corpses, if not the lust for power in the soul of man?

ANGELA   The patriarchal ideology *constructs* men obsessed with conquest and power, and your plays helped *legitimise* that obsession.

SHAKES   The lust for power is not 'constructed'! It is a demon all men are born with.

ANGELA   And woman aren't?

SHAKES   Yes but that demon in you is not so relentless. And are we not *all* born with the demons love, grief, guilt, anger, fear, scorn, loyalty, and hate! Do the 'Hopi Indians' laugh when their child is struck down? Did King Lear need an 'ideology' to 'construct' his grief?

            [ANGELA *looks up and there is* KING LEAR, *played by her grandfather* COL, *holding an imaginary Cordelia in his arms, scanning the faces of those around him.*]

LEAR   Howl, howl, howl, howl! O! you are men of stones:
            Had I your tongues and eyes, I'd use them so
            That heaven's vault should crack.

She's gone for ever.

[LEAR *goes down on his knees.*]

Why should a dog, a horse, a rat, have life,
And thou no breath at all? Thou'lt come no
more,
Never, never, never, never, never!

[SHAKESPEARE *leads* LEAR *away, looking over his shoulder at* ANGELA.]

COL AND GRACE'S LIVING ROOM

ANGELA *is with* MARTIN, SARAH, GRACE *and her aunts* JESSICA *and* MONICA. *They all look sombre. It is* COL*'s wake.*

MONICA   You always hear people say, 'He died peacefully. He died peacefully.'

JESSICA   They should have given him more morphine.

MARTIN   He was pumped full of the stuff. Someone like Dad doesn't just bow out peacefully.

MONICA   It was just horrible. Why do they let it go on and on?

SARAH   Let's not talk about it any more, please.

ANGELA   Was it really bad for him at the end?

SARAH   Angela. Grace has been through enough.

MARTIN   [*to* ANGELA] He suffered. It wasn't easy.

GRACE   I said to him, 'Don't hang on, it's no use.'

            [*Pause.*]

            He's at peace now.

MONICA	Thank God.
GRACE	The funeral was beautifully conducted.
JESSICA	Except for that unctuous minister.
GRACE	He spoke very well.
MARTIN	Mum he was awful. He didn't even know Dad.
MONICA	All he did was spout platitudes.
MARTIN	I should have spoken.
ANGELA	Yes.
GRACE	Ministers always speak at funerals. It's their job.
MARTIN	I should have spoken.
JESSICA	We all should have.
MARTIN	What would you have had to say that was in any way positive?
JESSICA	We all had our criticisms of Dad but we all loved him.
MARTIN	Pity he didn't see much evidence of it when he was alive.
GRACE	Martin, don't get upset. I was often very hurt about the way Jessica and Monica treated your father, but this is the time to forgive and forget.
JESSICA	*We* treated him? If there was any damage to be inflicted you led the pack.
GRACE	Jessica, don't be ridiculous. Your father and I loved each other for over fifty years.
MARTIN	I never would have suspected it.
GRACE	He was a terrible old bastard, but I still loved him.
JESSICA	Mum, he ridiculed anything we ever tried to do.
MONICA	I got as good a result as Martin in high school and he wouldn't let me go to University.

MARTIN   We've heard this dozens –

MONICA   Well it's true. I had to go and earn a living.

MARTIN   He was tough and hard, but he did love us.

JESSICA   [*to* MARTIN] I don't know why you're defending him. He was harder on you than anyone.

MONICA   You used to come inside some mornings and your hands would be bleeding he'd worked you so hard.

MARTIN   He was on the point of cracking up.

JESSICA   He could have hired someone. He was just too bloody mean.

MARTIN   Why did we bother with a funeral? We should have just dumped him in the harbour.

GRACE   I loved your father but he was a mean bastard, and no amount of glossing over can change that fact.

JESSICA   He *must* have more money stashed away somewhere.

MONICA   Has to be a fortune there. Has to be.

MARTIN   Sorry, I've been through everything and the net assets are the house and four thousand dollars and that's it.

JESSICA   I don't believe that. We've always known he had a hoard somewhere.

MONICA   We always thought that at least we'd get *something* one day.

JESSICA   There must be money. There has to be.

MARTIN   There isn't.

JESSICA   Then where the hell did it go?

            [ANGELA *cannot control her anger any longer.*]

ANGELA   He gave a third of what he earned to Billy Headen for nearly fifteen years.

[*They stare at her.*]

JESSICA   Pardon?

ANGELA   He gave a third of what he earned to Billy Headen for nearly fifteen years.

MONICA   That can't be right.

ANGELA   It is. I checked with Elsie Headen.

JESSICA   His family misses out on everything because he's giving it to the bloody Headens?

GRACE   I *knew* there was something fishy going on. I *knew* that Elsie bloody Headen was hiding something. Could never look me straight in the eye!

MARTIN   That makes an awful lot of things clear.

JESSICA   Yes, that he was prepared to sacrifice us for them!

MONICA   He must have been sleeping with her.

MARTIN   Who? Elsie Headen?

MONICA   Probably was. She could never look me in the eye.

ANGELA   Because she was embarrassed and guilty. She told me.

MONICA   So she bloody ought to be.

ANGELA   Col felt he had to help Billy, because Billy would have done it for him.

JESSICA   Typical. He'd make a hero of himself to the Headens but his own family come last!

ANGELA   I think that's really unfair.

MONICA   Angela, I know how emotional a funeral can be for someone your age –

ANGELA   Don't patronise me Monica! Grandad helped another family survive by an extraordinary act of generosity and none of you has *one* good word to say about him.

MARTIN   I have.

ANGELA   Well you didn't say it at the funeral when it counted!

SARAH   Angela, don't get yourself upset.

ANGELA   Do you know what he told me? He'd be glad when he
           died because there'd be nobody to blame for your
           misery but yourselves.

SARAH   Angela.

ANGELA   [*to* JESSICA*and* MONICA] And as far as you two are
           concerned he thought you should stop your bellyaching
           because you'd both done brilliantly.

JESSICA   Brilliantly?

ANGELA   [*to* JESSICA] You've been supported for by your ex
           husband for twenty years while you've expressed your
           inner artistic core, [*To* MONICA] and you've avoided the
           oppression of marriage and still had eight or nine trips
           around the world with your boss, while his unsuspecting
           wife stayed home with the kids.

ANGELA'S ROOM – LATER

ANGELA *is reading a manuscript when* SARAH *enters.* ANGELA *looks
up.*

SARAH   Feeling better?

           [ANGELA *smiles at her mother and nods.* SARAH
           indicates the manuscript she is reading.]

           What do you think?

ANGELA   I think it's good.

SARAH   So do I. I mean I don't think he's ever going to be another Raymond Carver, but I'm sure someone will publish it.

            [MARTIN *comes in and sees* ANGELA *holding the manuscript and goes to retreat.*]

ANGELA   Dad, come back. It's good.

            [MARTIN *reappears.*]

MARTIN   You're just saying that.

ANGELA   No, it's *much* better than the other one.

SARAH   See, I told you.

MARTIN   It's not boring?

ANGELA   No, it's very good.

MARTIN   It's still just a rough draft and the ending still needs a lot of work but I think that it does have a pretty gripping premise and it would be very filmable – not that I'm writing it with film in mind –

ANGELA   Now I've got you both here, could you two tell me something?

MARTIN   What?

ANGELA   Are you two just staying together because of me, because it you are, please don't.

            [MARTIN *and* SARAH *look at each other, puzzled.*]

            Well don't look so surprised. You're so resentful of each other. I don't want to think you're both enduring misery because of some misguided idea that I'll fall apart if you separate. I'm nineteen and quite capable of coping.

            [MARTIN *and* SARAH *look at each other again.*]

SARAH   We love each other.

[ANGELA *stares at them both.*]

ANGELA   You've been badmouthing each other to me since I was three.

SARAH   That's what children are for.

ANGELA   I've been experiencing a *good* marriage?

MARTIN   No, you haven't, we have.

SARAH   If it'd been a bad marriage you probably wouldn't have known a thing.

ANGELA   What do you *love* about each other? Let me in on the secret.

SARAH   Your father is gentle, considerate, he listens to my problems, which is more than you do – and when he's not feeling sorry for himself he's sometimes funny –

MARTIN   And your mother's courageous and indomitable and when she's not feeling sorry for herself she's quite funny herself only she doesn't usually realise it.

SARAH   Thank you dearest.

MARTIN   And your mother is surprisingly – no, forget that.

SARAH   Look Angela, don't think we're senile or starry eyed. If there had been a Petruchio around when your father was courting me –

MARTIN   Thank you. Well I'll tell you something, there were some slightly less assertive and very attractive young women around who *did* think I was something of a Petruchio.

SARAH   So why didn't you marry them?

MARTIN   You beat them up.

SARAH   I pulled one girl's hair because she was so bloody stupid. [*To* ANGELA] Look it's never perfect, but in any real marriage that's how things are.

THE TUTORIAL ROOM

SWAIN *waits in the tutorial room.* MELISSA *enters.* SWAIN *smiles at her and hands her a paper.*

SWAIN   A plus.

MELISSA   Thank you. I'm really – thrilled.

SWAIN   It was a fine piece of work. Congratulations.

MELISSA   That means that –

SWAIN   That means your final assessment is B minus for the course.

MELISSA   Yow!

SWAIN   Now that there's no *question* of impropriety, I think it's time you sampled my Moroccan couscous.

MELISSA   I don't think I'd better Grant. I've become rather seriously involved with a guy who tends to misinterpret that sort of thing.

SWAIN   I thought –

MELISSA   It just all took off last week. I didn't really think he was my type but something just – clicked.

SWAIN   Not that – not that swaggering rugby jock –

MELISSA   Just because Julian is a top athlete doesn't make him a moron.

SWAIN Not that loud, braying, insensitive, arrogant fool you introduced me to in the coffee shop?

MELISSA I find him very attractive.

SWAIN You've really made an idiot of me, haven't you?

MELISSA I'm sorry Grant, I don't really know what you're talking about. Are you implying that the marks you gave me weren't genuine?

SWAIN I've become extremely fond of you Melissa and I had thought the feeling was reciprocated.

MELISSA Are you saying the marks you gave me weren't genuine, because if you are –

SWAIN Of course they were genuine, but –

MELISSA Good marks equals sex. Is that what was going on in your mind?

SWAIN No! For God's sake this was not a case of exploitation. I have grown extremely fond of you!

MELISSA You're married.

SWAIN My marriage is a total disaster!

[ANGELA *enters.* SWAIN *makes a great effort to control his anger.* ANGELA *looks at* MELISSA. *She cannot help but notice a strong tension between* MELISSA *and* SWAIN.]

ANGELA Am I interrupting something?

MELISSA No, no. I'm just leaving.

[*She sweeps out leaving* SWAIN *simmering with fury.* STEVE *enters.*]

ANGELA Perhaps I should give this paper another time?

SWAIN No. No. Go ahead.

ANGELA You're sure.

SWAIN   Let's get it over. You only need a D to pass the course.

STEVE   What do I have to get for my final paper?

SWAIN   A plus.

STEVE   Merry Christmas.

             [*He turns to leave.*]

ANGELA   You're not going to even listen to mine?

STEVE   Other people's intelligence depresses me. No, that's mean spirited. I'll stay. Dazzle me.

SWAIN   If you've no interest in this course leave.

STEVE   I'll stay.

SWAIN   When you're ready Angela.

             [ANGELA *notices that* SWAIN *has literally begun to twitch with suppressed rage, but she has no option but to continue.*]

ANGELA   The proposition we have been introduced to this year is that ideology constructs our 'reality' and that 'human nature' and 'truth' are humanist fictions. When I talked to my family there was a lot of material that *supported* the notion their 'reality' *was* strongly influenced by ideology. My mother *does* see the world from a strong feminist viewpoint but she can still admit that she is on occasion attracted to, say, the swaggering macho mastery of – Petruchio.

SWAIN   I'm sure she is.

ANGELA   Sorry?

SWAIN   [*savagely*] Your average woman obviously finds 'swaggering macho mastery' far more attractive than mere intellect.

             [ANGELA *is taken aback by the intensity of* SWAIN*'s statement.*]

But what can you expect. The dominant culture pumps out incessant images of brainless jocks carrying balls over lines in order to divert a brainless population from understanding how totally manipulated they are. Go on, go on!

ANGELA   So yes, my mother sees the world ideologically, but she also perceives and acknowledges her own frailties and weaknesses.

SWAIN   Frailty, thy name is woman!

[SHAKESPEARE *appears. Unseen by all but* ANGELA.]

SHAKES   [*to* ANGELA] They all quote me in the end.

ANGELA   [*to* SWAIN] Sorry?

SWAIN   My wife Joanna. Swears she will not even *apply* for the position in Queensland because she loves me too much! Hah! Couldn't bear us to be parted! Hah! I get a letter in the mail this morning telling me it's all over. She's fallen in love with the Vice Chancellor. A hollow little ex-*engineer* whose only talent is posturing and strutting for the media! Sorry. Go on.

[ANGELA *looks at* STEVE. SWAIN *is showing every sign of becoming unhinged, but there is nothing much* ANGELA *can do but continue.* SWAIN *continues to twitch as the rage and resentment boils up inside him.*]

ANGELA   My father is to some extent trapped within the dominant ideology. He does feel a failure because he couldn't live up to its macho demands, but he's also warm, forgiving and tells funny jokes.

STEVE   He's a Liberal humourist.

ANGELA   My late Grandfather Col felt that if the patriarchy *was* controlling society, then in his case, it had certainly failed to deliver.

SWAIN   The patriarchy has never delivered power to all men.

It's the swaggering peacocks at the top that get everything! And idiot women, brainwashed by the dominant culture, chase them to the ends of the bloody earth.

STEVE   Women have always chased the guys with power and status. It's in their bloody genes.

SWAIN   [*semi hysterical*] Don't you *dare* even suggest a biological basis! I can see why you failed the course. Nothing is biological, nothing! It can all be reversed. If we take the dominant culture, expose it, rip it apart, then the peacocks, the strutters, the jocks will have had their day! The meek will inherit the earth!

SHAKES   [*shaking his head sadly*] The last person who espoused that belief ...

            [*He mimes being nailed on a cross.*]

ANGELA   If Shakespeare was alive today I think he would say there *was* a human nature and that the natures of men and women differ.

SWAIN   Of course he would, the strutting patriachal peacock!

ANGELA   I think he would say we are all born with inner demons –

SWAIN   Rubbish!

ANGELA   And that male demons shout 'power' louder than female demons.

SWAIN   Rubbish!

ANGELA   But after talking to my mother I think that if there *is* an average biological difference in the sexes' need for power, then it's not nearly as great as Shakespeare would have us believe.

SHAKES   Who kills and murders for power? Men!

SWAIN   Angela, I warn you that if you are suggesting there is *any* biological difference between male and female, it will not be tolerated! Are you suggesting that?

ANGELA   I'm saying I simply don't know!

STEVE   This isn't education, it's bloody indoctrination!

SWAIN   Education is *always* indoctrination. The question is to
             what ends. The feminist multicultural project will not
             tolerate any *hint* of biological determinism! There are *no*
             demons in the brain. Everything can be changed and
             will be changed! There are no demons! None!

SHAKES   Zounds the man is more dense than a pox brained
             whoreson!

SWAIN   Angela! Get that. None!

SHAKES   Men's brains are aburst with demons!

             [SHAKESPEARE *summons up a* JOANNA DEMON, *a* VICE
             CHANCELLOR DEMON *and a* PROFESSOR MEACHAM
             DEMON. *They are played by the actors who play*
             JESSICA, MARTIN *and* COL. *They appear in surreal half
             masks and ghostly half light.*]

SWAIN   Joanna. How could you do it? How could you go off
             with that cretin! Why have you humiliated me like this?

JOANNA   Ask *yourself* why, Grant.

SWAIN   You stole her, Mr *Vice* Chancellor! You lured her up
             there and stole her!

VC DEMON   No Grant, she came willingly. Very willingly. Ask
             yourself why.

SWAIN   It's your fault Meacham! If you hadn't blocked my
             promotion she would have stayed.

MEACHAM   I didn't block your promotion Grant. Your colleagues
             did. Ask yourself why.

SWAIN   [*to all of them*] Why?

ALL   [*in a loud repetitive chant, akin to a mantra*] Because you're a totally inadequate human being. Because you're a totally inadequate human being. Because you're a totally inadequate human being. Because –

SWAIN   [*covering his ears, screaming*] No!

[SHAKESPEARE *gestures and* SWAIN*'s* DEMONS *disappear. He resumes the scene unaware of what has just happened to him.*]

[*To* ANGELA] There are *no* demons in the brain. One hint of demons in the brain and you fail!

ANGELA   You're going to have to fail me in any case Grant. I'm quitting the class.

STEVE   Yoh!

ANGELA   The more I listened to the tapes of my family, the more convinced I became that there *is* a human nature and that it consists of more than just demons *or* ideology.

STEVE   Go Angela!

ANGELA   Human nature *must* have *something* to do with my Grandfather's compassion, my mother's courage, and with my parents' loyalty and love for each other –

SWAIN   Angela –

ANGELA   And it must have something to do with why the great writers like William Shakespeare can still speak to us across the ages. Grant, the world has a lot of problems, and I support feminism and multiculturalism, but what you're teaching isn't helping the world, or ethnic minorities, or women. It's a quarter truth elevated to holy writ, whose only function, frankly, seems to be an attempt to further the academic careers of middle-aged Anglo Celtic males.

STEVE   [*correcting her*] Middle-aged Anglo-Celtic male arseholes.

SWAIN   All right, if that's the way you want it, fail! Both of you. Fail! Scurry back to your tepid liberal humanism

and fail! Go grovel to your pathetic canon of Dead
White Males, but be sure of one thing – Grant Swain
will not grovel! Never! Tomorrow belongs to me!

STEVE   Dr Swain?

SWAIN   Yes!

STEVE   Go Foucault yourself.

[STEVE *leaves.* SHAKESPEARE *laughs at* SWAIN *'s
humiliation.*]

SWAIN   I haven't finished with you.

SHAKES   Then sir, do your worst!

[SWAIN *aims his gun.* SHAKESPEARE *grabs his arm. They
wrestle. The gun goes off.* ANGELA *moves forwards
anxiously.*]

SWAIN   One of us is shot.

SHAKES   The audience had'st best see whom.

SWAIN   For God's sake. This is the late twentieth century. No
one expects narrative closure.

SHAKES   'Tis my firm belief that a story must have a beginning,
middle and an end.

SWAIN   Shakespeare, you are so fucking out of date!

[SWAIN *limps offstage. He has shot himself in the foot.*]

SHAKES   Who sayest the power of metaphor is dead!

[SHAKESPEARE *turns to* ANGELA *triumphantly thinking
he has won.*]

ANGELA   William, you are a wonderful writer, but by and large
your women *are* a bloody disgrace. One of the greatest
actresses of our era, Glenda Jackson, had to leave the
stage and become a *politician* because the only role she
had to play in *your* repertoire was the nurse in *Romeo
and Juliet*!

SHAKES   [*claps his hand to his head*] Oh MiGod! I wish me back to an era of sanity.

ANGELA   Right away.

          [*She flicks her fingers and he is gone.*]

OUTSIDE THE TUTORIAL

ANGELA *and* STEVE *are together.*

STEVE   Well that's it I guess.

ANGELA   How do you feel?

STEVE   Actually? Great.

ANGELA   So do I. Who wants to end up with a Literature major and hate literature?

STEVE   I won't be ending up with anything.

ANGELA   Why not?

STEVE   I'm quitting the University. It's not my scene.

ANGELA   What are you going to do?

STEVE   I'm too embarrassed to tell you.

ANGELA   Tell me.

STEVE   I'm starting an apprenticeship. Mechanic.

ANGELA   If that's what you wan to do, fine.

STEVE   Yeah. See you.

ANGELA   Steve, would you like to come to a movie?

          [*He turns and looks at her.*]

STEVE   Which one?

ANGELA   Let's do it this way. You pick yours, I'll pick mine, we'll toss a coin, and go to mine.

          [STEVE *looks at her.*]

          It was a joke. I'm working on my sense of humour.

STEVE   It was good.

ANGELA   You didn't laugh.

STEVE   I thought you were serious.

ANGELA   Perhaps it's a bad idea.

STEVE   No, no. It's a great idea. Now let's just grab the entertainment guide, go to lunch and begin negotiations.

ANGELA   You think I'm difficult?

STEVE   Why would I ever think that?

ANGELA   I think it's important in any relationship that we do try and make ourselves aware of any vestiges of unconscious mind sets.

STEVE   I think that this could be the start of an endlessly intriguing – friendship.

          [ANGELA *looks at him earnestly trying to decide if he is being ironic. She decides he is, but lets it pass. This time. They walk off together. She reaches for his hand. Surprised, he takes it.*]

                              THE END

Selected References

Michael D. Bristol, *Shakespeare's America, America's Shakespeare,* Routledge, 1990.

Simon During, *The Cultural Studies Reader,* Routledge, 1993

Terry Eagleton, *Literary Theory, - An Introduction,* Blackwell, 1983

Peter B. Erickson, *Patriarchal Structures in Shakespeare's Drama,* University of California Press, 1985

Richard Freadman and Seumas Miller, *Rethinking Theory,* Cambridge University Press, Cambridge,1992

George Levine, *Constructions of the Self,* Rutgers University Press, 1992

Madan Sarup, *Post-Structuralism and Postmodernism,* Harvester Wheatsheaf, 1993

Elaine Showalter (ed) *The New Feminist Criticism,* Virago, 1986

Gary Taylor, *Reinventing Shakespeare,* The Hogarth Press, 1990

Chris Weedon, *Feminist Practice and Poststructuralist Theory,* Blackwell, 1987

Keith Windschuttle, *The Killing of History,* Macleay, 1984